THE COMPLETE PRESSURE COOKER COOKBOOK

THE COMPLETE PRESSURE COOKER COOKBOOK

120 easy, everyday recipes and key techniques

Sam & Dom Milner
of KitchenGadgetsClub

WHITE LION PUBLISHING

Quarto

First published in 2026 by White Lion Publishing
an imprint of The Quarto Group.
One Triptych Place,
London, SE1 9SH
United Kingdom
T (0)20 7700 6700
www.Quarto.com

EEA Representation, WTS Tax d.o.o., Žanova ulica 3, 4000 Kranj, Slovenia
www.wts-tax.si

A catalogue record for this book is available from the British Library.

HB ISBN 978 1 83600 645 9
PB ISBN 978 1 83600 646 6
Ebook ISBN 978 1 83600 647 3

10 9 8 7 6 5 4 3 2 1

Designer: Georgie Hewitt
Project Editor: Jo Roberts-Miller
Food Photographer: Dan Jones
Appliance Photographer: Alison Field
Food and Prop Stylist: Sophie Mackinnon
Food Stylist's Assistant: Sadie Albuquerque
Group Publishing Director: Denise Bates
Senior Editor: Nicky Hill
Senior Designer: Renata Latipova
Senior Production Controller: Rohana Yusef

Printed in Guangdong, China TT/September/2026

MIX
Paper | Supporting responsible forestry
FSC® C016973
www.fsc.org

Notes

- All calorie counts are per serving where a recipe states 'Serves' or per item when a recipe states 'Makes'
- Metric and imperial measurements are given for all recipes, use one set only and not a mixture of both
- All tablespoons and teaspoons are level unless stated
- All milk should be whole/full-fat unless otherwise stated
- All eggs should be UK large eggs or US XL eggs, unless otherwise stated
- Be careful when handling raw chicken, never wash it and never use anything that has come into contact with it, i.e. utensils and chopping boards, on cooked foods, without washing them thoroughly first
- When baking sweet treats, we recommend unsalted butter, and in savoury cooking salted butter.
- Do refer to your electric pressure cooker manual, as they often operate differently, and follow the manufacturer's safety guidelines
- Do not place the pressure cooker on top of a hot surface/hob/stovetop, or in a heated oven
- Do not place food/liquid in the pressure cooker when the cooking pot is not inside it. You don't want the heating element to get damaged
- Keep a safe distance away from the pressure cooker when releasing pressure
- All recipes in this book use high pressure only

CONTENTS

INTRODUCTION

I remember the date well in my head – 25 November 2016. It was our daughter Sofia's second birthday. Jorge was a newborn baby. And we were adding a new kitchen gadget to our collection. The Instant Pot electric pressure cooker.

We already had a kitchen full to bursting with kitchen gadgets. We had our trusted air fryer that was well past its best thanks to its over use, our soup maker, bread maker, ice cream maker (we lived in Portugal at the time so that was a must!), two slow cookers and a redundant oven.

We loved the idea of combining electric pressure cooking and air frying, to see how they would sit next to each other in our Portuguese kitchen. We loved the idea of cooking the main protein in one and the sides in the other. Very soon we were cooking salmon and broccoli in the pressure cooker and potatoes in the air fryer. It was the perfect pairing.

It's hard to believe that was almost a decade ago. Sofia is going to be twelve in a couple of months and Jorge is now ten. They have grown up to love the pressure cooker like we do and always cheer that dinner is ready when they hear that familiar beeping sound.

Like most people learning a new type of cooking, we made mistakes. But we found favourite recipes and, as we cooked more and more things, our confidence and love for the pressure cooker grew. At the same time, we developed a pressure cooker community and we learnt from each other.

In this pressure cooker cookbook (OMG our fourth book!) we are going to walk you through pressure cooking from expert know-how to the water test, and zero-minute cooking to which pressure release to use and why, as well as sharing delicious pressure cooker recipes with you.

But, if you are one of the many people who have an electric pressure cooker sitting there collecting dust, then we hope this book will give you the enthusiasm and a bit of our passion to get started and fall in love with the pressure cooker, like we did. You'll find plenty of tips and tricks throughout this book to help you learn a new way of cooking.

Love Sam & Dom x

PRESSURE COOKING 101

WHAT IS A PRESSURE COOKER?

A pressure cooker is a kitchen gadget that uses high pressure steam to cook food rapidly. For example, a whole chicken would roast in a preheated oven in 1 hour 50 minutes, yet the same chicken would cook to a pull-apart texture in 39 minutes plus 'time to pressure' (more on this on page 13) in a pressure cooker.

WHY PRESSURE COOK?

The three main reasons people love pressure cooking is speed, hands-free cooking and better nutrition. They fall in love with how much faster certain foods cook (even professional chefs). Condensed milk to caramel is possible in just 35 minutes and that Christmas pudding can be cooked in 1 hour 30 minutes. Others love that they can walk away from the cooking pot, unlike with a stovetop pressure cooker. And then there are those who are not bothered particularly by nutrition, but fall in love with healthy foods because they love the process of pressure cooking it and how easy it is. For example, I had never cooked dried beans or lentils before I got my first pressure cooker, but I was excited to cook dried haricot beans, rather than relying on a can of beans in tomato sauce.

THE 1960S PRESSURE COOKER

I love snuggling on the sofa with Sofia watching a girly movie. She is a girly girl and has beautiful brown hair, brown eyes and loves a sleeping mask at nighttime, which reminds me of Audrey Hepburn's character in *Breakfast At Tiffany's*. So, as you can imagine, that movie is often on. We were watching it together on a cold winter's day and one scene really grabbed our attention. She is cooking dinner and she is distracted. The stovetop pressure cooker lid flies off and she simply says to the guy, let's go and eat out instead.

I am an 1980s baby so the 1960s pressure cooker was just something I know about from movies. But our community have also told us how they have a fear of modern pressure cookers because of what happened to them in the 1960s! Whenever I mention this to Sofia, she can't believe we're talking about the same thing, as electric pressure cookers have been part of her mealtimes for the last 10 years.

THE MODERN ELECTRIC PRESSURE COOKER

While the 1960s pressure cooker is thought of with fear and stories of explosions and food on the ceiling, it's a totally different story when it comes to the modern electric pressure cooker. You can be relaxing, scrolling on your phone or watching TV while it's on, in a similar 'set and forget' way that you use a slow cooker or air fryer. Just listen for that familiar beep when it is done and you can release the pressure and finish making the recipe.

It's also nice to have a digital screen, as with your other gadgets, so you can plan your time efficiently to know when dinner will be done.

THE UNEXPLAINED 1%

Occasionally things don't go to plan, though – perhaps a recipe you've made a zillion times fails to go to pressure and you see the burn warning. Simply add a little extra liquid, stir and reset the cooking time.

You might be wondering why this happens and how often it happens. Well, we call it the unexplained 1%. For every 100 things you cook under pressure, one will frustrate you and just not go according to plan. You might have done everything right, so you just have to put it down to one of those annoying things.

Behind the scenes here, while we were making this pressure cooker book, we proved the 1% theory! If you think that an average cookbook has 100 recipes, working on that 1% rule, we would expect 1 of those 100 to fail. The fail at our photoshoot was peri peri chicken and rice. During our recipe testing it was some broccoli – we've cooked broccoli in the pressure cooker more than 1,000 times but for some reason on that occasion it failed!

So, if you do have an occasional failure to pressure, you are not alone. If it happens more often than 1%, though, consider doing the water test on page 12 to make sure you don't have a major issue.

FROM STOVETOP TO ELECTRIC PRESSURE COOKING

One of our readers called Rudi is a big fan of pressure cooking and was over the moon when he heard we were making this book. He has German heritage and, as Germany was early to the pressure cooker, I've always been fascinated with his cooking stories. His mum started with the Ritter Kochlust 10 litre (10.5 quart) stovetop pressure cooker in 1952, after giving birth to his little sister. I love that, like us, having a baby was her starting point. She used it most often for potatoes, veg, meat, cake and fruits in season, and Rudi watched food being made in the stovetop pressure cooker throughout his childhood and well into adulthood. He then made the swap from stovetop to electrical. If you're wondering just how different they are, my biggest takeaway from talking to Rudi and others is that you don't need to babysit electric pressure cookers, and they have other functions too.

Throughout the book you'll see a mixture of quick pressure, natural pressure and delayed pressure. This is the biggest change from old-fashioned pressure cookers, which only had natural pressure release. Our generation has a choice, and we can delay release for perfect meat, or go fast so we don't overcook our veg.

THE MANY ELECTRIC PRESSURE COOKER MODELS

Over the last 10 years, we have watched as pressure cooker brands have tweaked their design to match customer needs and what their loves and loathes are. They've added an automatic release option for those who don't like releasing the pressure through fear of the steam, and they've made it possible to set the delayed release time, rather than having to keep an eye on the time yourself.

We've based the recipes in this book around the Instant Pot Duo 6QT/5.7 litre because it's the one we have had the longest. And, because it doesn't have the bells and whistles of newer pressure cookers, it's a great one to learn from.

Recipes in this book have also been tested using: Instant Pot Duo 8QT/9.1 litre; Ninja Foodi 9-in-1; Ninja Foodi Max 15-in-1; and Instant Pot Duo Crisp.

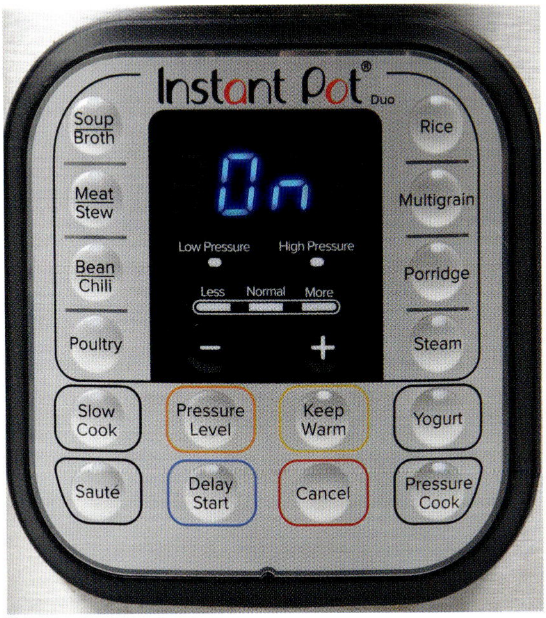

GETTING THE PRESSURE COOKER OUT OF ITS BOX

When people start pressure cooking, the first thing they talk about isn't the great taste or the quick cook, it's the fear. The fear that it won't go to plan and it won't work for them. But there isn't anything to worry about, if you remember the rules: use enough liquid for the food to go to pressure but not too much that you have a dishwasher, watery soup; don't use liquids that are too thick, such as a jar of pasta sauce, unless diluted; don't fill the cooking pot past the max line; and cook ingredients together that have a similar cooking time.

So, just get going and you'll realise that pressure cooking is not as hard as you might think. Have a flick through the book and plan your firsts. But, most importantly, get the pressure cooker out of the box!

Our go-to beginner recipes are:

Condensed milk caramel page 212
Frozen broccoli page 145
Brown rice page 110
Whole chicken page 50
Chicken fajitas page 166
Prawn pil pil page 82
Carrot & ginger soup page 124

THE 12 STAGES OF PRESSURE COOKING

When you're a beginner, pressure cooking can seem like a lot to get to grips with but, in reality, the method of pressure cooking always stays the same.

01 Add food to the cooking pot.
02 Add enough liquid to bring the food to pressure.
03 Secure the lid.
04 Set the valve to sealing.
05 Press pressure cook.
06 Set the cooking time.
07 The pressure will build up.
08 Pressure cooking time starts.
09 Delayed release if needed.
10 Move the valve from sealing to venting.
11 The pressure releases.
12 Remove the lid.

Travelling with your Pressure Cooker

Pressure cookers, especially the medium ones, such as the Instant Pot Duo 6QT, have become very popular for travelling. They are not as powerful as the modern multicooker and use just 1,000 watts. This makes them ideal for use at campsites and on the road in a motorhome or caravan.

In the summer of 2018, we travelled around eight countries in Europe. At the time, the kids were sixteen, twenty-one months and three-and-a-half years. We used the pressure cooker for every meal and even used it as a way to warm up Jorge's milk bottles and to boil the water for coffee. Looking back years later, what we loved was that it was almost half the wattage of an air fryer so we never tripped the fuse of the campsite and, best of all, we could make delicious meals and have a budget holiday. Also, the cooking pot is rather big and, to save on travelling space, we often fill it with our favourite accessories!

If you have a motorhome or similar, it's perfect for taking with you and you can make any of the recipes in this book. Our go-to recipes were usually pasta dishes or soups made with ingredients we had bought from local markets.

THE BUTTONS YOU'LL SEE ON ALL ELECTRIC PRESSURE COOKERS

Pressure cook
You'll obviously use this button the most. On really old models, it's called manual. You then can set the cooking time.

Sauté
You'll find yourself using this a lot, whether to cook the onion and garlic first, or to reduce a sauce after pressure cooking. Think of it as an electric hob/stovetop. It gets hot fast and stays hot, so be careful you don't burn the garlic.

Slow cook
Pressure cookers all come with a slow cook function. Some love it, some hate it. I rarely use it because I just love that pressure cooking is fast.

Keep warm
If you have an older pressure cooker, they will often move to this setting automatically when on a delayed release/natural release. You can also use this setting if you've made dinner but are not quite ready to eat.

Delayed start
This is great if you are planning on eating later. You can prepare the dish and it will start when you are ready.

+ and -
This is how you adjust the cooking time. You can also use this if you need to go from high pressure to low pressure.

High or Low Pressure
Earlier pressure cookers didn't have a low setting and everything was high. In this book you won't have to worry as there are no recipes using low pressure.

Start/cancel
Some models are automatic and will start as soon as you've set the cooking time, so you don't have to press a start button. It simply varies. In other models, you have to press start to get them going. But all models have a cancel button. Simply press cancel after the total cooking time, including any delayed or natural pressure release, otherwise it will stay on to keep warm. Many varieties will also have presets – these are preset cooking times for different foods, such as beans, soup, rice and poultry. Because the cooking times needed can differ greatly, depending on quantities and ingredients, most people rarely use them. Don't worry if you feel like you're not making use of all the buttons.

Remember to Press Cancel

A big error that people make is forgetting to press the cancel button when they are done. If you don't press cancel after pressure cooking, it will stay on 'keep warm.' This means that, if you go to have dinner and the pot is empty and just needs washing up, it's like keeping an empty pot on a hot stovetop.

You must also remember to press cancel when you have finished sautéing. The cooking pot gets hot very fast and stays hot, too, so it's always best to cancel a little before you really need to. If you leave it turned on after sautéing with nothing in the pot, it's likely to go to the HOT screen and it will take longer to clean.

THE WATER TEST (AND WHY YOU MUST DO IT)

Now, this often confuses people when they get a pressure cooker. They are told they must do what is called a water test before they cook real food. The reason for this is that you need to check the sealing ring, not just the pressure cooker as a whole. You need to make sure it's attached properly and your food is going to go to pressure. Remember, the way pressure cooking works is that it uses high-pressure steam, so a water test checks that you can create the required high-pressure steam.

01 To complete the water test, simply pour warm water from the hot tap until it reaches 3 litres/3.2 quarts in your cooking pot.

02 Secure the pressure cooker lid and set the valve to sealing.

03 Pressure cook for 2 minutes, followed by a quick pressure release.

04 Remove the lid – if you have boiling hot water (be careful!), your pressure cooker has passed the water test.

You also now have a sterilised cooking pot (perfect if you didn't buy it brand new) and you know your sealing ring is working. You can start pressure cooking.

We also recommend doing the same test before making jam (see page 44) or 2-ingredient yoghurt (see page 40), in order to sterilise the pot.

Help! My Pressure Cooker isn't Going to Pressure!

Another occasion when the water test might be repeated is when you're cooking food and it keeps failing to go to pressure. If you've made the same food a few times and, all of a sudden, there's no pressure, then do the water test. It might be that the sealing ring is not working. If it doesn't go to pressure with the water test, you change the sealing ring and do the water test again. If it now goes to pressure, you know it was the sealing ring that was the problem.

Needing to replace the sealing ring is something that can happen at any time. That's why on page 20 we recommend having a spare sealing ring among your pressure cooker accessories kit. We made the mistake of not having a spare and had to get one sent to a campsite we were staying at when we were travelling!

Freezing, Batch Cooking & Vegetarian Pressure Cooking

When you flick through the recipes in this book, you'll notice a set of symbols at the bottom of each recipe. These show you when a recipe is freezer friendly, good for batch cooking or vegetarian friendly. Instead of just including everything that is freezer safe, we have only included freezing and batch cooking foods that would still taste just as good if you freeze them or if you have them as part of a batch-cooking session. When freezing or batch cooking, we recommend you read the useful information in our Cook Once, Eat Twice chapter and that you freeze and batch your go-to recipes and build up a freezer collection over time.

Freezer friendly **Batch cooking** **Vegetarian friendly**

HOW LONG DOES FOOD TAKE TO GO TO PRESSURE?

Now, this is the big question. You know how long the pressure cooking time is. You know what the release time is. But you'll rarely see in any cookbooks the time it takes to go to pressure.

This is because there is no one standard time for all pressure cookers: the altitude can make it vary; the brand of pressure cooker can alter it (some are higher wattage and more powerful than others, which can make a big difference); and how much food you are cooking makes a difference (for example, it's much quicker to get to pressure when you cook brown rice or broccoli than a big pot of beef and barley stew).

You can also find that if you have a pressure cooker that is very quick to get to pressure, the food won't be as done compared to a slower one.

We recommend you do our 'Time to Pressure Test', so you can compare how your pressure cooking performs using 3 different recipe types.

You can see our time taken to pressure with both the Instant Pot Duo 6QT and the Ninja Foodi Max 15-in-1. **Note we have found the larger the pressure cooker, the longer it takes to go to pressure.**

Half a butternut squash using the tall trivet/rack.

Instant Pot Duo 5 minutes to pressure
Ninja Foodi 15-in-1 8½ minutes to pressure

A large whole chicken on a trivet/rack.

(We followed our 'How long to cook a whole chicken' guide on page 50.)

Instant Pot Duo 13 minutes to pressure
Ninja Foodi 15-in-1 14 minutes to pressure

A big pot of leftover beef and barley soup.

(The plan was to reheat the soup from page 70 for dinner but the pressure cooker was rather full so it's an interesting experiment. The more liquid in the cooking pot, the longer it takes to go to pressure. The butternut squash and the whole chicken are going to be much quicker because of this.) Each pressure cooker was filled to 4 litres/4¼ quarts in liquid volume and all 4 litres needs to warm up, boil and go to pressure. Much more than the 240ml/1 cup liquid for the butternut squash or whole chicken.

Instant Pot Duo 30 minutes to pressure
Ninja Foodi 15-in-1 31 minutes to pressure

THE 4 TYPES OF PRESSURE RELEASE

As you read through the recipes in this book you will see mentions of different pressure releases. But what do they all mean and what is the difference?

Quick pressure release

Also known as QPR, this is when you press cancel, move it from sealing to venting and release the pressure as soon as the food has finished pressure cooking. This is essential for quick-cooking food, such as frozen broccoli on page 145. What you have to appreciate, however, is that it can still take a few minutes to release the pressure before you can safely remove the lid.

Delayed pressure release

Also known as DR, this means exactly what it says. It is when you delay releasing the pressure. This delay can vary from recipe to recipe (15 minutes for a whole chicken; although, with more delicate foods, it's a much quicker delayed release as every second counts, as shown with tuna on page 80). What it does, though, is continue the cooking process at a much lower pace. This cooking time is important, though, and without it your food is either not as tender or undercooked. Depending on your pressure cooker type, you can either set the release time automatically or keep track by counting up – we use Alexa!

Natural pressure release

Also known as NPR, this can make a recipe feel like it's taking forever to finish. NPR means leaving the food sitting there in the cooking pot until the pressure has released on its own. There are very few recipes in this book that use a full natural pressure release – one is the jam on page 44. As a general note, foamy foods that are likely to spit, foam up or expand during cooking, require a natural release, such as jams/preserves or sauces.

Controlled/pulse pressure release

Also known as CR, this means releasing the pressure gradually in short bursts. We use this for the creamy chicken gnocchi soup on page 130. Some pressure cookers have a pulse release and are able to do this automatically for you. You're controlling the release for foods that are likely to spit as you release the pressure. You may wonder why you don't just do a longer delayed release. The reason is, the food is done and you don't want it to continue cooking.

Understanding which to use

We often get asked which pressure release is best and whether there is a general rule for which one to use.

Quick Release When you need things done very precisely and leaving it even 1 minute longer will affect the result. This often applies the most to veg.

Controlled Release If you are cooking something and it's very starchy or is going to have a very hot liquid. It's generally a food that is likely to overcook with a natural release, such as gnocchi soup or meatballs.

Delayed Release When you want the food to sit there a little longer. You are essentially using the cooking pot as a steamer to keep cooking the food at a slower rate. This is good for joints of meat, such as gammon, whole chicken etc., because it makes it tender. However, with rice and pasta, a delayed release is planned into the cooking time and, without it, it would be undercooked.

Natural Release This is the cautious setting, for foods that you want to make sure are cooked in the middle, such as steamed puddings, or for foods you know are going to be dangerous to release, such as jam, because hot syrup could go all over your kitchen!

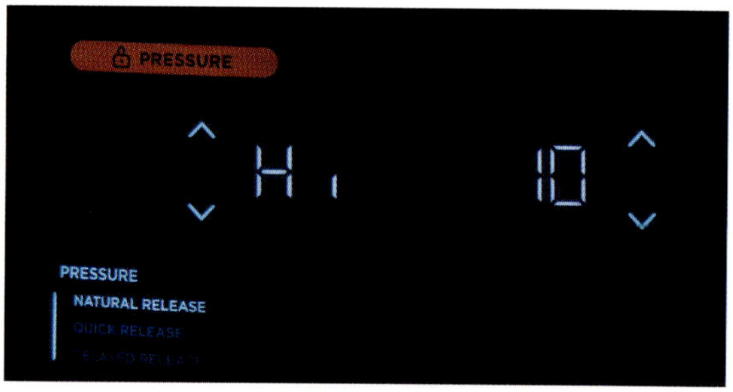

ZERO-MINUTE PRESSURE COOKING EXPLAINED

Now, this throws every beginner when they first hear it. How can you cook for 0 minutes?! Surely there needs to be a number of minutes? With microwaving, air frying, slow cooking etc. you always have a cooking time. So, what gives?

When you cook with a pressure cooker, the total cooking time is actually made up of a few different stages, each measured in time:

The time to pressure

This is the time it takes for the food in the cooking pot, with the valve set to sealing, to reach pressure.

The cooking time at pressure

This is the cooking time that you set to cook the food, and will be the cooking time after it has gone to pressure.

The release time

This is the time after cooking, when you leave the pressure cooker to release naturally, or have a controlled release, or for a delayed release.

The venting time

This is the time it takes for the steam to be released, once the valve has be turned to vent. The more liquid in the cooking pot to begin with, the longer it takes. For example, it's a long wait for a big pot of soup or stew, but is quite quick for rice.

Now, with a zero-minute cooking time, you only have the time to pressure and the venting time. Simply adjust the cooking time all the way down to zero, then press start. Below are some examples using zero-minute pressure cooking time.

Zero-minute Recipes

Cheesy Prawn Linguine
(see page 104)

Triple Cheese Mac & Cheese
(see page 106)

Broccoli & Cauliflower Cheese
(see page 146)

Egg Roll in a Bowl
(see page 170)

Dirty Water Dogs
(see page 75)

Make-ahead Vegan Bean Ragu
(see page 97)

Red Onion Gravy
(see page 139)

Zero-minute Frozen Broccoli
(see page 145)

YOUR PRESSURE COOKER QUESTIONS

What does 'going to pressure' mean? You will hear this expression a lot. 'Gone to pressure' simply means that the pressure cooker has heated to the point where the liquid inside is turning into steam, which creates high pressure inside the pot.

What does sealing versus venting mean? These are the different positions for your valve at the top of your pressure cooker. Sealing is the position you need to place it in for the pressure cooker to go to pressure. When it has finished cooking, you release the pressure by changing the valve to venting – the steam can then be released.

What happens if I forget to set the valve to sealing? As the steam builds, it will release out of the cooker, without any pressure being created. As soon as you realise your error, move the valve to sealing. Don't worry, many pressure cooker veterans forget to set the valve to sealing and have to go back to the pressure cooker to double check and flick it over!

Do you always use sealing? Sealing is used for pressure cooking only. You don't need it when you are steaming, sautéing, slow cooking or making yoghurt.

What is a sealing ring? It is made of silicone and without it your pressure cooker won't go to pressure. It is situated in the lid, so you are unlikely to notice it at first. Depending on how much pressure cooking you do, it can last from 3 months to 2 years.

My sealing ring stinks. What should I do? Leave the lid open in between cooks, so it's not left closed with the smell increasing. And you can give it a good clean. Letting it soak in a sink full of cold water with a dishwasher tablet can also make a difference.

What is a BURN warning? You may see the capital letters – BURN – come up on your cooking pot screen. This means the cooking pot is very hot and the food has caught on the bottom and is burning the bottom of your cooking pot. This can easily be fixed. Simply press cancel, remove the lid and inspect the food. Usually this happens when the pot runs out of liquid and it's like it has boiled dry. Add some more liquid, give it a stir, then secure the lid back on, set the valve to sealing and set your cooking time.

What does HOT mean? Sautéing in a cooking pot is often compared to using an electric hob/stovetop. They get hot fast and can take a bit of time to cool back down. When the display shows HOT it's important you press cancel, take it off the heat and leave it to cool down. Otherwise, you will have a cooking pot to soak because of food burnt onto the bottom, and it will struggle to go to pressure.

What does PRE mean? The instant pot brand will say ON when the cooking time starts. But over at Ninja they instead have PRE, which is an abbreviation for preheating.

What does L000 mean? This stands for lapse time. It's the time counting up, once the main pressure cooking time finished. Let's say a recipe calls for a 5-minute delayed release, the screen will go to L000 when the cooking time has finished and it starts the delayed release, then you should press cancel when it says L005.

Can I pressure cook without the cooking pot? No, absolutely not. Underneath the pot is where the electrics are for your pressure cooker and it's very dangerous if any liquid gets in this area. If this area gets wet by accident, make sure it's fully dry before adding the cooking pot and cooking again.

Help! My pressure cooker releases steam as it goes to pressure This is perfectly normal – they all lose some steam as they go to pressure.

How do I know when the pressure has finished releasing? Most models have a metal float valve that drops when pressure has finished releasing. More modern pressure cookers will show DONE or END on screen to indicate it is done. Another clue is that you aren't able to open the lid on electric pressure cookers until the pressure is fully released.

Help! My pressure cooker never went to pressure This can happen from time to time. It's because the pressure cooker needs to build up steam to get pressure from the liquid. This can happen if there isn't enough liquid in the pot and if it's dried out. Remove the lid, check the liquid and, if needed, adjust the level and stir. It can also happen if the liquid is too thick.

Other reasons are: the sealing ring needs replacing; or the cooking pot has lost its non-stick coating. If it continues to happen, complete the water test as instructed on page 12.

What is deglazing the cooking pot? You will often see deglazing mentioned after sautéing but before pressure cooking. It is the process of pouring liquid into the cooking pot after a sauté to stop it burning and to release any food stuck to the bottom. Press cancel after sautéing, add liquid, stir and scrape any stuck bits with a wooden spoon. If you don't do this, it can result in the BURN warning and failing to go to pressure.

What liquid can you use when you pressure cook? Any thin liquid that won't stick to the cooking pot can be used – wine, water and stock are all popular options. Unless extra water is added to make them thinner, gravy, passata and canned tomatoes are a bad choice.

Why do most recipes use cold liquid? Pressure cooking is a science, in the same way as baking, and the time it takes for the liquid to come to pressure is included in the cooking time. If you use boiling hot stock, it will go to pressure more quickly and the food will be under cooked.

Is there a maximum liquid quantity? Yes, but this varies depending on the size and shape of your cooking pot. For example, our Instant Pot Duo 6QT has a maximum of 4 litres/4¼ quarts, whilst our Ninja Foodi 15-in-1 has a maximum of 6 litres/6.34 quarts.

I have an Instant Pot Duo 6QT does that mean I can add 5.5 litres of liquid? No. While the whole cooking pot is 5.5 litres/5¾ quarts, it has a maximum liquid quantity of 4 litres/4¼ quarts, which gives it 1.5 litres/6½ cups of pressure-cooking space.

If I double the ingredients, do I double the cooking time? No, it stays the same. Even if you make 3 times the quantity, you still cook for the same cooking time. However, it will take longer to go to pressure, because there is more food in the cooking pot.

Can I cook frozen meat or fish in the pressure cooker? Yes! You will need to add extra cooking time to make up for the food being cooked from frozen. I have found meat is just as delicious cooked from frozen. You will find a recipe for whole frozen chicken on page 53 and frozen tuna on page 80, for example.

What size pressure cooker should I get? There are 3 popular sizes: 3 quarts, 6 quarts and 8 quarts. I think of them as feeding 1–2, 2–4 or 4–6 people. Consider your household size when planning which one to get. Note that if you want to cook a turkey crown/bone-in turkey breast or other large cuts of meat and poultry, the 8-quart pressure cooker would suit you best. As a family of 5, we find the 6 quart is perfect. One problem with the smaller size is that there are fewer accessories made for it, because it's less common. For example, you can't use most trivets or the egg bite mould because they don't fit in the 3-quart pressure cooker.

Why do we sometimes recommend frozen garlic & ginger? The cooking pot gets hot fast and it's so easy to burn chopped garlic and ginger. By swapping it for frozen, you're slowing down how quickly it cooks.

Is there food to avoid in the pressure cooker? The pressure cooker is very fast cooking, so any food that is very delicate is likely to spoil. Pressure cooked food has a soft texture, like slow-cooked food, so you won't achieve the desired texture if you're expecting something crispy.

Is the slow cooker any good? If you speak to a group of pressure cooker veterans, the room will be divided when it comes to the slow cooker function on their pressure cooker. Some will love it, some will hate it, and some will have owned a pressure cooker for years but never slow cooked in it. From personal experience, I find that it differs greatly between manufacturers. Some are great, some are okay and some are dreadful. Some will automatically set it to very low and you'll need to adjust the temperature to high before slow cooking. Most, though, will be 20 per cent slower than slow cooking in a traditional slow cooker. So, for example, if you'd normally slow cook for 4 hours on high, it would take 5 hours.

Can you slow cook with these recipes? Yes, most recipes are slow cooker friendly. In fact, the Christmas gammon on page 62, the teriyaki chicken noodles on page 60 and the chicken casserole on page 188, are all favourite recipes converted from the slow cooker to the pressure cooker. We haven't included slow cooker recipes here because some brands of pressure cooker have a very, very slow low. By that we mean if you pressed low on a regular slow cooker, your food would be ready in 7–8 hours, but with some electric pressure cookers, this can be 12–14 hours.

WHAT YOU NEED TO PRESSURE COOK

This is our go-to list of pressure cooker accessories. The accessories you use the most will depend on what you like to cook. We've built our collection over time, so we recommend getting them as you need them.

Cooking/inner pot Depending on the brand, this is referred to as either a cooking pot or an inner pot. I find both names have great logic. It's what you cook your food in. The inner pot describes it well because it's the inside pot that sits on the heating element. Throughout the recipes, we call it the cooking pot, though.

Sealing ring The pressure cooker can't seal and go to pressure without a sealing ring. A new pressure cooker will usually have one fitted. They need replacing regularly – how often will depend on how often you use it.

Metal trivet/rack If you're not cooking food directly in the bottom of the cooking pot, you'll need a trivet/rack. Pressure cookers usually come with one, and the kind of trivet/rack will depend on the brand. It's great if you want to stack food or if you want a steam-like result. The trivet is often smaller and perfect for holding chicken breasts or a whole chicken. A rack is usually flat and better for pork chops or salmon.

Tall trivet We were early to the Instant Pot UK crowd, so we were waiting a while before accessories arrived in the UK. The tall trivet was very much worth waiting for – it allows you to cook one food in the cooking pot and another above it. This is our favourite pressure cooker accessory.

Trivet with handles This is another trivet favourite. Many trivets are flimsy and hard to get in and out. If you have one with handles, it's much easier to lift.

Hot pan stand You often need to remove the cooking pot, to prevent the BURN warning and to stop food from continuing to cook. But the pot is very hot and you don't want to burn your kitchen worktop. We have an old, round chopping board – emphasis on old, as you don't want a mark on your favourite board – to put the hot pot on.

Springform tin/pan Frittata, cheesecake and key lime pie, for example, all work wonderfully in an 18cm/7in springform tin.

Mesh strainer We use this for straining yoghurt, rinsing rice and for straining the tiny bones from stock.

Silicone oven mitts These are really handy for grabbing the cooking pot without burning yourself. If you're browsing through all-in-one pressure cooker sets, you often see these included.

Silicone egg mould This is a 7-egg-shaped mould used to make sous-vide-inspired egg bites and omelette bites. They are also brilliant for little desserts, too. We have lots of different recipe ideas using them in this book.

Measuring cups and spoons An essential part of our pressure-cooking kit. Many ingredients are easier to measure in cups and there are often teaspoon or tablespoon quantities, too. There are many varieties of measuring cups and spoons, but my favourites are plastic ones for measuring olive oil, rice and pasta, and metal ones for dried herbs and spices.

Expandable steamer basket I love this as it works in any pressure cooker because it expands to fit, and it works well for pressure cooking vegetables.

Ceramics, glassware and silicone Ramekins, mini casserole dishes and other similar bakeware that fit in your cooking pot are a great addition. Ramekins are great for small bakes and casserole dishes are perfect for cooking from frozen and your Cook Once, Eat Twice leftovers. Glassware and silicone can be used in the same way. We like silicone because it cleans so easily afterwards.

Pudding basins Sweet and savoury steamed puddings work well in the pressure cooker – see our Christmas pudding for sweet on page 206 and beef Bourguignon pudding for savoury on page 192.

Meat claws Because pressure cooking creates very tender poultry and meat, meat claws are a must-have. They are perfect for pulled chicken, pork and beef, and even for your next batch of chicken fajitas (see page 166).

SOUPER CUBES
SOUPER CUBES

Peeler A good peeler is an essential part of kit – peeling potatoes for mash, peeling carrots for stew . . . A good peeler always helps.

Wooden spoons You don't want to use metal spoons in the cooking pot, as the pot scratches easily. Wooden spoons are brilliant for everyday use. Expert tip – buy 35cm/14in wooden spoons. Cooking pots are deep, and a long spoon will prevent you burning yourself and makes stirring easier.

Tongs These are very handy for turning food and removing meat from the cooking pot.

Freezer bags, labels and pens Pressure cooking has long been associated with batch cooking – a big portion of soup, a big pot of Bolognese, or a big hearty stew with plenty of leftovers. We recommend heavy-duty freezer bags, good labels and chalk pens. Chalk pens are a batch cooker's best friend, as they write well and don't smudge afterwards.

Freezer cubes We recommend using freezer cubes alongside freezer bags. Freeze leftovers into cube trays and, once they are frozen, transfer them to freezer bags to free up the freezer cube trays.

Spare sealing ring This is the accessory we recommend every pressure cooker owner has on standby. You need a sealing ring for food to go to pressure, and they all eventually stop working and need replacing. You don't know when that will happen, though, so it's a good idea to have a spare one ready.

Thermometer I can't imagine cooking without one of these and some pressure cookers have them built in. When you are cooking and experimenting with recipes it's a great way to make sure food is cooked through, or that the food you have reheated is at a safe temperature.

Sarah's Pressure Cooker Cleaning Tips

We asked Sarah our kitchen gadget cleaning expert and our recipe tester for pressure cooker cleaning tips and this is what she recommends. . . Most of the time she washes the pressure cooker and its accessories like any other pot or pan – hot soapy water, her favourite non-invasive kitchen cloth and some elbow grease.

To clean the outside of the pressure cooker, unplug it and turn it off first. To keep it clean and shiny, and to get rid of all those fingerprints, use any antibacterial spray or kitchen spray and a cloth, and wipe it clean.

For the rim where the cooking pot and the main unit meet, use the same method. Spray onto a cloth and wipe around. If you feel bits stuck that you can't reach, roll up a cloth to create a thin long tube, which is perfect for getting into those hard-to-reach areas.

For the inside lid, we recommend spraying some degreaser on a cloth and wiping, then wiping it off with a clean cloth. Also note, if you pressure cook a lot of veg, because your cooking pot is not that full, it will be like you are sterilising and deep cleaning the sealing ring and lid each time. This is because of all the pressure steam that is rising. This will be good enough most of the time. But sometimes your pressure cooker will be overly dirty or, just like an oven, will seem like it needs an extra special clean.

Our favourite method is a pressure clean. Add 960ml/4 cups cold water to the cooking pot. Drizzle in 2 teaspoons washing up liquid. Secure the pressure cooker lid, then pressure cook for 12 minutes, followed by a full natural pressure release. This cleans the cooker by boiling the water, going to pressure and giving it a thorough clean without any effort from you. Carefully pour away the boiling hot dirty water, give it a quick wipe and you'll have a very clean pressure cooker.

PRESSURE COOKING IS ALL ABOUT THE LIQUID

I was asked during the making of this book whether you need water to go to pressure every time? And the answer is YES.

This is very important, and beginners to pressure cooking don't often realise it. Even if you're cooking PIP (pot in pot), you still need liquid in the main cooking pot for it to go to pressure. It's this liquid that boils to create the pressure and the steam that you lock into the cooking pot. It also mainly needs to be cold (think cold tap, if using water) because the cooking time takes into account the time it takes to warm up.

You can choose between water, stock, wine, cider or other liquids, such as apple juice. Water is what you generally use if you're not cooking the food directly in the liquid, such as when you're cooking some veg on the trivet or if you're making jacket potatoes. If you're cooking food directly in the liquid, such as when you're making stews, soups, casseroles and pasta and rice dishes, you can use stock, to add flavour to the food.

Avoid thick liquids, though (such as passata, pasta sauce, salsa, milk, cream etc.), as it can be hit and miss whether it will go to pressure. You'll notice recipes in this book that use these ingredients either add them after pressure cooking or water them down, so they're not as thick (see the steel cut oats with coconut milk liquid on page 38).

You need a minimum quantity of liquid, too, and this can be annoying when you want to make only a small amount of food. Let me explain: 240ml/8½fl oz/1 cup always goes into the cooking pot (or 360ml/12fl oz/1½ cups for 8 quart pressure cookers – do check with your manufacturer, though, as it can vary depending on the shape or size of your cooking pot). There needs to be a 1cm/½in depth of liquid lining the bottom of the cooking pot so it can start preheating and eventually go to pressure.

This minimum quantity works with most food – from cooking a whole chicken to making a cheesecake. And you don't need to increase the liquid beyond the minimum level, even with large portion sizes. You can cook as little as 1 broccoli floret or as many as 30 broccoli florets without adjusting the liquid. This makes it great for adapting recipes from feeding 1 to feeding 6.

However, imagine you're cooking rice, pasta, lentils or beans – they all need the correct ratio of liquid to ingredient. Because of the minimum quantity of liquid to go to pressure, you can't just cook a tiny portion of rice for one person for lunch. With 240ml/8½fl oz/1 cup liquid in the cooking pot, you will need 200g/7oz/1 cup rinsed jasmine rice.

THE LIQUID RULE BREAKERS

You will see a lot of recipes in this book and online, too, that ask for 240ml/8½fl oz/1 cup of liquid to go to pressure. This is the standard quantity, unless you are making rice (see page 110), cooking beans or lentils (see page 90), or cooking dried pasta (see page 104), where it might need more, as the food expands as it cooks.

You will also see other recipes where you add more liquid, such as for a casserole, soup or a stew. This is because you want to make a bigger portion, or you want to get the ratio of other ingredients to liquid just right.

However, there are some rule breakers that go the other way – i.e. need less than the 240ml/8½fl oz/1 cup. This stresses people out, because we all have engrained in us the rule that it must be a minimum amount of liquid and if we don't, we'll break our pressure cooker. Well, let me explain two recipes which break the rules . . .

Homemade Jam/Preserve (see page 44)

There is no liquid added to these recipes at all. Not even a tablespoon of water! This is because the liquid to pressure comes from the juice of the fruit. So, if you are making a raspberry jam, all the juice comes out of the raspberries to get it to pressure and the fruit goes super soft.

Teriyaki Chicken Noodles (see page 60)

This is a pressure cooker hack. It uses 120ml/4fl oz/½ cup water in the base of the cooking pot. This stops it from sticking before the other ingredients are added. Then we add a thick sauce to it, which on its own at the bottom would fail to go to pressure, but adding on top of the water without stirring will mean it does. Then the sauce drops down into the water, and what you've really done is water down your sauce.

EGGS

LET'S BEGIN WITH PRESSURE COOKER EGGS

In November 2016 when we purchased our first electric pressure cooker, the biggest obsession was making hard-boiled eggs. It was the first thing everyone tried to cook in their pressure cooker - a bucket list recipe. You could see how amazing your pressure cooker was, get confident with it and tell the world you just pressure-cooked eggs! There were Facebook groups with millions of members all giving the newbie to the group a big thumbs up after they shared the pictures of their first perfectly peeled, pressure-cooked eggs.

But it was also a kind of scientific formula - 555. It sounded a bit confusing, if you'd just bought a pressure cooker, but it was a code that was loved by pressure cooker veterans. Firstly, let me explain exactly what 555 means, then we can begin your pressure cooker journey.

5-5-5

5-5-5 is the shortened form of the 3 cooking times that make the easiest-to-peel hard-boiled eggs:

5-minute pressure cook
5-minute delayed release
5-minute ice bath

HARD-BOILED EGGS

MAKES 7

PREP 5 MINS

SAUTE 0 MINS

PRESSURE COOK 5 MINS

RELEASE DR

TOTAL COOK TIME 5 MINS

68 CALS PER EGG

7 large eggs

01 Pour 240ml/8½fl oz/1 cup cold water into the cooking pot, then add the egg holder or trivet/rack. Carefully place the eggs in the holder/trivet.

02 Secure the pressure cooker lid and set the valve to sealing. Pressure cook for 5 minutes, followed by a 5-minute delayed pressure release.

03 Carefully remove the eggs and place them in an ice bath. Set a kitchen timer for 5 minutes and leave the eggs in the water until the timer beeps.

04 Tap the top and bottom of the egg shells on a clean worktop, then roll the eggs to make them easy to peel. Peel the eggs one by one, and you'll have hard-boiled eggs ready for serving!

Do You Love a Soft Yolk? Swap the 5 minutes pressure cooking for 2 minutes, then perform the same 5-minute delayed release and 5-minute ice bath.

Do You Love Dippy Eggs on a Weekend? Swap the 5 minutes pressure cooking for 0 minutes, followed by a 5-minute delayed release - no ice bath required!

TOP TIPS

Egg Holder This is a piece of kitchen equipment that is just for the pressure cooker. It's made of stainless steel and you slot the eggs into the holes, before placing the holder in the pressure cooker. It produces the best, evenly cooked eggs because the eggs wobble around less in an egg holder than they do in a steamer or trivet.

Steamer or Trivet If you don't have an egg holder, you can use the trivet that comes with the pressure cooker or a steamer basket. The trivet is better, as it is more sturdy and the eggs won't move about as much when cooking.

1 to 7 Eggs You can cook 1 to 7 eggs at the same time in the pressure cooker, without changing the cooking time.

MAKES
7

PREP
10 MINS

SAUTE
0 MINS

PRESSURE COOK
0 MINS

RELEASE
N/A

TOTAL COOK TIME
0 MINS

138 CALS

SOFIA & JORGE'S DEVILLED EGGS

This has become a Milner family Easter tradition that came about because we needed to find a way to use all the boiled eggs we'd cooked when we originally tested the pressure cooker boiled egg recipe. We let the kids loose with food colouring on the egg whites for fun and ended up with a snack, healthier than the usual chocolate and pastries.

- 7 large hard-boiled eggs (see page 24)
- 4 heaped tbsp light mayonnaise
- ¼ tsp mustard powder
- ½ tsp dried chives
- 28g/1oz/⅓ cup grated mature/sharp Cheddar
- 2 spring/green onions
- A couple drops of 3 different food colourings

01 Carefully slice the eggs in half and scoop the yolks into a medium bowl with a teaspoon.

02 Add the mayonnaise, mustard powder, chives, cheese and three-quarters of the spring onions to the egg yolks. Season generously with salt and pepper, and mix with a fork.

03 Fill 3 ramekins three-quarters full with cold water, then add a couple of drops of food colouring to each ramekin, placing a different colour in each one. You can mix and match (see below). If you want a deeper colour, add a few extra drops.

04 Place an egg white half in one of the ramekins of coloured water, leaving it for a couple of minutes until it has taken on a nice colour. Repeat with the remaining egg whites.

05 Pat the egg whites dry with kitchen/paper towel, then transfer to a serving dish. Spoon or pipe the egg yolk mixture into the egg whites. Sprinkle with the remaining spring onions before serving.

COLOURFUL DEVILLED EGGS

Rainbow Eggs A perfect activity for younger kids – let them decide which colours they want to use and let them mix and match.

St Patrick's Day Use bright green for your next 17 March Irish celebration.

Easter Mix and match your favourite Easter colours, from yellow chick, to green grass and other pastel spring hues.

Halloween You could make pumpkin orange, purple shades or spooky black.

Christmas Try Christmas-tree green, bauble red, or why not do a mixture of both?

Out of all these holidays, my kids look forward to the colours of Halloween the most. This is a good way to get them to eat some protein before trick or treating!

SERVES
6

PREP
2 MINS

SAUTE
0 MINS

PRESSURE COOK
12 MINS

RELEASE
QPR

TOTAL COOK TIME
12 MINS

110 CALS

THE FAMOUS EGG LOAF HACK

If there is a recipe hack for the electric pressure cooker that excites people the most, then it's the egg loaf. Imagine you're making egg mayonnaise and need loads of eggs but can't be bothered to peel them . . . Crack all the eggs into a container, pressure cook and you have this egg loaf. Chop, add mayo and you've got it without any peeling.

Olive oil spray, for greasing
7 large eggs

01 Pour 240ml/8½fl oz/1 cup cold water into the cooking pot, then add the trivet/rack. Grease a 18cm/7in round silicone container with a little olive oil to stop it sticking. Crack the eggs into the container one by one. Carefully lower the container onto the trivet inside the cooking pot.

02 Secure the pressure cooker lid and set the valve to sealing. Pressure cook for 12 minutes, followed by a quick pressure release.

03 Carefully remove the container from the cooking pot and set aside to cool.

04 Loosen the edges of the egg loaf with the tip of a round-bladed knife, if necessary. Place a dinner plate over the egg loaf, then flip the container over. Leave the container upside down over the plate for a couple of minutes and the egg loaf will drop out on to the plate.

05 Slice the egg loaf to serve. Mix with mayonnaise, if using for egg mayonnaise, or serve as it is – perfect for salads and great for meal prep.

MAKES
7

PREP
5 MINS

SAUTE
0 MINS

PRESSURE COOK
10 MINS

RELEASE
QPR

TOTAL COOK TIME
10 MINS

104 CALS

EGG BITES MASTER RECIPE

Egg bites have become world famous thanks to coffee shops. They are a healthier option to have with your coffee instead of a cheese toastie/grilled cheese or a slice of cake. In a nutshell, they are like a mini frittata but, instead of being fried, they are cooked in a pressure cooker in egg bite moulds. They have a similar texture to sous vide cooking. As they are similar to a frittata, any favourite frittata filling will work. They keep well in the fridge and are perfect for meal prep and taking to work, for picnics or school packed lunches.

Olive oil spray, for greasing
4 large eggs
250g/9oz/1 cup ricotta cheese
1 tsp dried parsley

01 Pour 240ml/8½fl oz/1 cup cold water into the cooking pot, then add the trivet/rack. Grease each of the 7 holes of the egg bite mould with a little olive oil to stop them sticking.

02 Crack the eggs into a bowl and add the ricotta. Sprinkle with the dried parsley and season generously with salt and pepper. Stir well with a whisk until creamy.

03 Divide the mixture between the 7 moulds, then secure the lid of the mould firmly in place. (This prevents hot steam from the pressure cooker dripping in and making the eggs watery.)

04 Lower the silicone mould onto the trivet inside the cooking pot. Secure the pressure cooker lid and set the valve to sealing. Pressure cook for 10 minutes, followed by a quick pressure release.

05 Carefully remove the mould from the trivet, then remove the lid from the mould and set the bites aside to cool.

06 Loosen the edges of the egg bites with the tip of a round-bladed knife, if necessary. Place a dinner plate over the egg bites, then flip the mould over. Leave the mould upside down over the plate for a couple of minutes and the egg bites will start to drop out on their own. Gently squeeze any that haven't fallen out. But it's a game of patience – if you rush, they will come out like scrambled eggs!

TOP TIPS

Lower the Calories Swap ricotta for low-fat cottage cheese. You'll need to pulse the mixture in a blender to get the right consistency, though.

The Keto Way Another favourite combination is half cottage cheese and half double/heavy cream.

Meal Prep Hero That is how we describe egg bites. You can batch cook them and keep them in your fridge in your favourite Tupperware. They'll keep well for 3 days.

Let Them Cool Remove the lid and let them cool before tipping them out. Otherwise, they are likely to break up.

No Peel Boiled Eggs Instead of whisking the eggs and pouring them into the moulds, crack an egg into each hole. Pressure cook for 10 minutes, and you'll get egg-bite-shaped boiled eggs.

Buying Silicone Moulds You can buy them in different sizes and with different lids – silicone or plastic. We find the silicone lid is longer lasting. The dimensions are: 20 x 19 x 5cm (8 x 7½ x 2in).

7 EGG BITE FLAVOURS

Go beyond the master recipe with these delicious flavour suggestions. Simply choose one or do a mixture. Use the master recipe from page 30 for the cooking time and method. Avoid wet or fatty added ingredients, as you don't want your egg bites watery. Any uncooked add-ins should be cooked first, such as peppers, sausages etc. You can do a mixture, so if you want to do some asparagus, and some cheese and onion at the same time, you can.

Low-cal Red Pepper Egg White Bites Swap 4 large eggs for 6 large egg whites and use cottage cheese instead of ricotta. Add ½ finely chopped cooked red pepper to the batter.

Asparagus & Gouda Add 85g/3oz/¾ cup grated gouda cheese and 3 cooked asparagus spears that have been chopped into chunks to the batter.

Cheese & Ham This classic egg bite is made by chopping 3 slices ham into chunks and adding it to the batter with 55g/2oz/½ cup grated mature/sharp Cheddar.

Cheese & Onion Sauté 3 peeled and thinly sliced shallots with a little olive oil. Add them to the batter along with 55g/2oz/½ cup grated mature/sharp Cheddar.

Garlic & Veg Add 115g/4oz cooked frozen veg (with excess liquid removed), and 1 teaspoon each of garlic purée and dried oregano to the batter.

Sausages & Bacon Sauté 2 sausages and 2 rashers of bacon (with the bacon fat removed) with a little olive oil. Thinly slice, then pat dry with kitchen/paper towel to remove excess grease. Add to the batter.

Marry Me Peppers Sauté a thinly sliced yellow pepper with a little olive oil. Add it to the batter with a teaspoon each of smoked paprika and sun-dried tomato paste. Sprinkle in 2 tablespoons grated Parmesan.

MAKES
7

PREP
8 MINS

SAUTE
5 MINS

PRESSURE
COOK
10 MINS

RELEASE
QPR

TOTAL
COOK TIME
15 MINS

161 CALS

Olive oil spray, for greasing
100g/3½oz/¾cup plain flour/all-purpose flour
55g/2oz/generous ¼ cup granulated sugar
1 tsp ground cinnamon
1 large egg
300ml/10½fl oz/1¼ cups whole/full-fat milk

BLUEBERRY SAUCE

170g/6oz/1 cup blueberries
2 tbsp granulated sugar
2 tsp vanilla extract
1 tbsp maple syrup or runny honey

BLUEBERRY PANCAKE BITES

With a simple pancake batter and blueberry sauce, you have pancake bites in your egg bite moulds. As this is simply a fun-shaped pancake, you can mix and match with any of your favourite pancake toppings. Whilst I love this blueberry sauce, it's also nice to have them with some leftover strawberry coulis from page 204.

01 Pour 240ml/8½fl oz/1 cup cold water into the cooking pot, then add the trivet/rack. Grease each of the 7 holes of the egg bite mould with a little olive oil to stop them sticking.

02 To make the batter, in a medium bowl, add the flour, sugar and cinnamon. Crack in the egg and mix with a fork. Gradually pour in the milk, beating the mixture all the time with a fork.

03 Divide the mixture between the 7 moulds, then secure the lid of the mould firmly in place. (This prevents hot steam from the pressure cooker dripping in and making them watery.)

04 Lower the silicone mould onto the trivet in the cooking pot. Secure the pressure cooker lid and set the valve to sealing. Pressure cook for 10 minutes, followed by a quick pressure release.

05 Carefully take the mould out of the cooking pot, remove the lid and set the egg bites aside to cool.

06 In the meantime, make the blueberry sauce. Place the blueberries, sugar, vanilla and 4 tablespoons water in the cooking pot. Press sauté and sauté the blueberries until softened. Press cancel and leave to cool a little.

07 Loosen the edges of the egg bites with the tip of a round-bladed knife, if necessary. Place a dinner plate over the egg bites, then flip the mould over. Leave the mould upside down over the plate for a couple of minutes and the egg bites will start to drop out on their own. Gently squeeze any that haven't fallen out. But it's a game of patience – if you rush, they will come out like scrambled eggs!

08 Serve the bites with the blueberry sauce and a drizzle of maple syrup or runny honey.

Yorkshire Pudding Meets Pancake Bites During recipe testing for this book, we made a plain pancake batter using the same ingredients that traditionally go into Yorkshire pudding. We cooked them using the times above and they tasted just like a Yorkshire pudding but had the texture of a muffin.

COURGETTE BREAD BITES

MAKES
7

PREP
5 MINS

SAUTE
0 MINS

PRESSURE COOK
12 MINS

RELEASE
QPR

TOTAL COOK TIME
12 MINS

160 CALS

Now that we've shown you a sweet bite, how about transforming your classic courgette bread into bites? This batter is so easy to make, the bites taste delicious and they are perfect for meal prep. Courgette bread bites, or zucchini bread to our Australian and American/Canadian readers, are just as delicious as the original bread. Think about all the other bread bites you could make – pumpkin bites at Halloween, gingerbread bites at Christmas, or hot cross bites for Easter.

- Olive oil spray, for greasing
- 1 large egg
- 4 tbsp extra virgin olive oil
- 1 tsp vanilla extract
- 50g/1¾oz/¼ cup granulated sugar
- 2 tbsp soft brown sugar
- 85g/3oz courgette/zucchini
- 90g/3¼oz/⅔ cup self-raising/self-rising flour

01 Pour 240ml/8½fl oz/1 cup cold water into the cooking pot, then add the trivet/rack. Grease each of the 7 holes of the egg bite mould with a little olive oil to stop them sticking.

02 Crack in the egg into a medium bowl, add the olive oil and vanilla, and beat with a fork. Add both sugars and continue to mix. Grate the courgette into the bowl (no need to squeeze the excess moisture out), then stir. Mix in the flour until you have a thick batter.

03 Divide the mixture between the 7 moulds, then secure the lid of the mould firmly in place. (This prevents hot steam from the pressure cooker dripping in and making them watery.)

04 Lower the silicone mould onto the trivet inside your cooking pot. Secure the pressure cooker lid and set the valve to sealing. Pressure cook for 12 minutes, followed by a quick pressure release.

05 Carefully take the mould out of the cooking pot, remove the lid and leave the egg bites to cool.

06 Loosen the edges of the egg bites with the tip of a round-bladed knife, if necessary. Place a dinner plate over the egg bites, then flip the mould over. Leave the mould upside down over the plate for a couple of minutes and the egg bites will start to drop out on their own. Gently squeeze any that haven't fallen out. But it's a game of patience – if you rush, they'll come out like scrambled eggs!

BREAKFAST

FOUR SEASONS STEEL CUT OATS

SERVES 6

PREP 2 MINS

SAUTE 0 MINS

PRESSURE COOK 14 MINS

RELEASE DR

TOTAL COOK TIME 14 MINS

289 CALS WITHOUT THE TOPPINGS

200g/7oz/1 cup steel cut/pin head/Irish oats
1 x 400g/14oz can coconut milk
4 tbsp granulated sugar

SPRING CHOCOLATE

40g/1½oz dark chocolate chips
4 tsp Biscoff spread

SUMMER FRUITS

200g/7oz mixed summer fruits (we use blueberries and raspberries)
4 tsp runny honey
2 tsp sunflower seeds

AUTUMN PUMPKIN SPICE

1 tsp pumpkin spice
1 tbsp maple syrup
2 tsp chopped dried cranberries
2 tsp pumpkin seeds

WINTER GINGERBREAD

¼ tsp ground mixed spice
1 tsp ground ginger
2 pinches of ground nutmeg

I first tried porridge in the pressure cooker whilst on night feeds breastfeeding Jorge. He's ten now! The appeal was being able to dump just two ingredients into the pressure cooker and leave it to it, then have something filling I could reheat when I was hungry.

The best oats to pressure cook for porridge/oatmeal are what they call pin head oats in the UK, Irish oats, or steel cut oats in the US. They take longer to cook, have a slight bite to them, even when cooked, and hold up well when adding flavours and other ingredients. If you pressure cook regular oats, it can be hit and miss with going to pressure and they can stick a fair bit. But pin head oats have a thicker texture, which makes them a better pressure cooker option.

We have 4 flavour combinations for spring, summer, autumn and winter. Follow the master recipe then choose one variation.

01 Add the oats to the cooking pot and pour in the coconut milk.

02 Refill the can with cold water and shake it about to loosen the last bits of coconut milk stuck to the sides, then pour this in too. Half fill the can for a final time and add this.

03 Secure the pressure cooker lid and set the valve to sealing. Pressure cook for 14 minutes followed by a 10-minute delayed release.

04 Sprinkle in the sugar, add your seasonal ingredients and give it a good stir with a wooden spoon. Let it sit for a couple of minutes before serving, as it will thicken up naturally.

HOW TO PRESSURE COOK YOGHURT

With over 120 recipes in this book and a fridge packed with leftovers as we test everything, the food the kids and the grown-ups fight over most is the pressure cooker yoghurt. It tastes authentic and expensive, like yoghurt you'd have at a nice restaurant in Greece.

So, it's no wonder it's the number 1 most-talked-about food among new pressure cooker users and the recipe still talked about fondly by pressure cooker veterans. Whenever we make it, we always say, why don't we do this more often?

Include it as an ingredient, eat it plain, or use it as the base and flavour it as you would a shop-bought yoghurt. On page 42 we show you how to use the yoghurt for your own strawberry protein shakes.

2-INGREDIENT EVERYDAY YOGHURT

SERVES 4
PREP 15 MINS
YOGHURT COOK 8 HRS
PRESSURE COOK 2 MINS
RELEASE QPR
TOTAL COOK TIME 8 HRS 2 MINS

234 CALS

- 2 heaped tbsp yoghurt with active cultures (we use thick full-fat Greek yoghurt)
- 1.9 litres/64fl oz/8 cups UHT/fairlife/long-life milk (we use semi-skimmed/2%)

This is the yoghurt master recipe. Mix it with your favourite fruit, go Greek with some honey, or add caramel or chocolate bits for the kids.

01 Sterilise the cooking pot first by adding 3 litres/3.17 quarts of cold water to the pot and pressure cooking for 2 minutes, followed by a quick pressure release. Empty out the cooking pot and you are ready to make yoghurt.

02 Add the yoghurt to the cooking pot, along with 240ml/8½fl oz/1 cup of the milk. Start mixing it with a whisk until frothy. Gradually add the remaining milk, whisking as you add.

03 Secure the pressure cooker lid but don't set to sealing. Press the yoghurt setting, then press the arrow down to fermentation and set the time to 8 hours.

04 When it has beeped and you have finished the 8-hour yoghurt cycle, don't stir. Cover the cooking pot with a silicone lid or wrap tightly in foil, and transfer to the fridge. Let it chill for 8 hours.

05 After 8 hours, remove the yoghurt from the fridge and set up your straining system. There's no need to buy lots of extra equipment for this, you just need kitchen/paper towel and a mesh strainer.

06 Place the mesh strainer/sieve over a bowl, then line it with kitchen paper/paper towel. Pour some of the yoghurt into the lined strainer – just until it is full. In about an hour, it will have strained through the kitchen paper and into the bowl. Repeat until all the yoghurt is strained. I normally leave it going in the kitchen as a background task while I cook other things.

07 Once strained, the yoghurt is ready for serving.

UNDERSTANDING THE YOGHURT AND THE MILK

What Are Active Cultures and Why Are They Important? To make yoghurt, a starter culture (active culture) is needed to begin the fermentation process in warmed milk. Active cultures ferment lactose (milk sugar) into lactic acid. This acid causes milk proteins to thicken, creating the characteristic creamy texture and delicious flavour.

What Is the Best Yoghurt to Use? We found that authentic Greek yoghurt works the best and produces the creamiest yoghurt.

Why Long-life milk? It has undergone ultra-high temperature treatment (UHT), so all the bacteria has been killed off and you don't need to pasteurise the milk before making yoghurt.

STRAWBERRY PROTEIN SHAKES

SERVES
1

PREP
5 MINS

SAUTE
0 MINS

PRESSURE COOK
0 MINS

RELEASE
N/A

TOTAL COOK TIME
0 MINS

252 CALS

250g/9oz/generous 1 cup homemade yoghurt (see page 40)
1 tbsp strawberry protein powder
2 tsp maple syrup or honey
1 tsp vanilla extract
55g/2oz strawberries

You made the yoghurt, now let's transform it into delicious protein shakes. These make a great on-the-go breakfast or snack.

01 Place all the ingredients in a blender and blend until smooth.

02 Pour into your favourite glass or shake holder.

03 Enjoy immediately, or chill in the fridge until later, if you're planning to drink it on the go.

Mix & Match If you don't have strawberry protein powder, you can still make the shake and it will be delicious. It would also work with chocolate, plain or vanilla protein powder, instead.

KIDS' CARAMEL YOGHURTS

SERVES
2

PREP
5 MINS

SAUTE
0 MINS

PRESSURE COOK
0 MINS

RELEASE
N/A

TOTAL COOK TIME
0 MINS

277 CALS

3 heaped tbsp dulce de leche caramel (see page 212)
250g/9oz/generous 1 cup homemade yoghurt (see page 40)

The kids love to add caramel to homemade yoghurt. Think delicious caramel or toffee yoghurt but cheaper as you're making it at home. It's also a great use of the condensed milk you turned into caramel on page 212.

01 Drizzle some of the caramel around the bottom and sides of 2 jars.

02 Divide the yoghurt between the jars, then stir in the remaining caramel. Chill until ready to serve.

Caramel Yoghurt Ice Cream Add the caramel yoghurt to ice lolly moulds and freeze overnight. You'll have delicious caramel yoghurt lollies/popsicles.

HOW TO PRESSURE COOK JAM/JELLY

Dom talks fondly about his time in catering college training to be a chef. He always says that he learnt soup first, then he made a lot of jam – lots of different jam flavours in a big pan. So, when we got our original pressure cooker, it was one of the first foods he wanted to see remastered the pressure cooker way. We were amazed to find that you didn't need pectin or other ingredients to thicken classic jams.

You can mix and match the master recipe to use other similar fruits – blueberry and strawberry are among our favourites.

Also to note – the time of the year when you are making your jam will affect the result. For example, you'll find it thickens more quickly out of season when the fruit is not as juicy. Think summer strawberries vs winter strawberries.

DOM'S 2-MINUTE RASPBERRY JAM

MAKES 3 JARS

PREP 8 MINS

SAUTE 0 MINS

PRESSURE COOK 2 MINS

RELEASE NPR

TOTAL COOK TIME 2 MINS

31 CALS PER TABLESPOON

Let's start our jam making with raspberry. It has only a 2-minute cooking time and is so easy. No need for pectin or adding any other thickening ingredients.

- 800g/1lb 12oz fresh raspberries
- 700g/1lb 9oz/3½ cups granulated sugar
- Juice of 1 medium lemon
- 1 tbsp runny honey

01 Sterilise 3 large or 6 small jam jars.

02 Add all the ingredients to the cooking pot and give them a good stir.

03 Secure the pressure cooker lid and set the valve to sealing. Pressure cook for 2 minutes, followed by a full natural pressure release.

04 Open the lid and blend about half of the raspberry syrup using a stick blender, then stir. This will help make the jam more smooth.

05 Carefully transfer the jam to the sterilised jars and chill overnight in the fridge.

DOM'S BLACKBERRY JAM

MAKES 3 JARS
PREP 8 MINS
SAUTE 0 MINS
PRESSURE COOK 2 MINS
RELEASE NPR
TOTAL COOK TIME 2 MINS

30 CALS PER TABLESPOON

800g/2lb fresh blackberries
700g/1lb 9oz/3½ cups granulated sugar
Juice of 1 medium lemon
1 tbsp runny honey

When blackberries are in season, Dom makes delicious jam with them. It's another easy 2-minute jam recipe and is the perfect ingredient to use in your baking, as well as to have on your toast for breakfast.

01 Sterilise 3 large or 6 small jam jars.

02 Add all the ingredients to the cooking pot and give it a good stir.

03 Secure the pressure cooker lid and set the valve to sealing. Pressure cook for 2 minutes, followed by a full natural pressure release.

04 Open the lid and blend about half of the blackberry jam syrup with a stick blender, then stir. This will help make the jam more smooth.

05 Carefully transfer the jam to the sterilised jars and chill overnight in the fridge.

HOW TO STERILISE JARS

You can use the pressure cooker to sterilise your jam jars. Simply place jam jars on a low trivet/rack without the lids and pour in 960ml/32½fl oz/4 cups cold water. Secure the pressure cooker lid and set the valve to sealing. Pressure cook for 2 minutes, followed by a quick pressure release.

THE BIGGEST PRESSURE COOKER MISTAKE WE EVER MADE!

The first time we ever made pressure cooker jam back in 2017, we guessed that doing a delayed release or a natural pressure release was unnecessary. So, after making raspberry jam for the first time, we did a quick pressure release. Well, that jam syrup squirted out as it released pressure and I had to move the kids swiftly out of the way. We had raspberry-coloured kitchen walls and I vowed never to make the same mistake again when making jam!

In this chapter we have 2 types of jam – both of them use a full natural release. However, we don't use a natural release with the lemon curd (see page 46) because that is cooked in jars so doesn't need it.

MAKES
1 LARGE
JAR

PREP
8 MINS

SAUTE
0 MINS

PRESSURE
COOK
12 MINS

RELEASE
DR

TOTAL
COOK TIME
12 MINS

25 CALS PER TABLESPOON

75g/2¾oz/⅓ cup unsalted butter
200g/7oz/1 cup granulated sugar
2 large eggs, plus 2 large yolks
1 tsp vanilla extract
6 medium lemons
1 tbsp plain/all-purpose flour

DOM'S LEMON CURD

This lemon curd brings back memories of Portugal for me. We lived there when we got our first electric pressure cooker, and we had a lemon tree in the garden. So, of course, lemon curd was the first recipe from the jam family that we made.

01 Sterilise 1 large or 2 small jam jars.

02 Place the butter and sugar in a mixing bowl and, using an electric hand mixer, whisk until the sugar and butter are well mixed. Note – it will be nice and soft but it won't be creamy like cake batter.

03 In a separate bowl, beat the eggs and the extra yolks, then add them to the butter and sugar mixture. Mix well with the hand mixer for a couple of minutes, until you have a gritty but combined mixture.

04 Add the vanilla extract and the grated zest of 2 of the lemons, and mix again. Add in the juice of all the lemons and mix lightly with a fork.

05 In a small bowl, combine the flour with 3 tablespoons water until smooth. Add this to the bowl with the lemon mixture and give the ingredients one last mix.

06 Pour the lemon curd into the sterilised jam jars and place the lids on top, but don't screw them tight (just one turn will do).

07 Pour 480ml/17fl oz/2 cups cold water into the cooking pot, then place the trivet/rack on top. Arrange the jam jars on the trivet.

08 Secure the pressure cooker lid and set the valve to sealing. Pressure cook for 12 minutes, followed by a 5-minute delayed release.

09 Open the lid and use a fork to stir the lemon curd while the jars are still in the pressure cooker, then leave them to cool for an hour in the pot. Secure the lids and transfer to the fridge. Chill for 12 hours before using.

Lemon Juice As we all know, some lemons are juicier than others. With a recipe like lemon curd, you want to get the lemon juice quantity spot on. We measured our lemon juice as we squeezed the lemons and achieved 10 tablespoons lemon juice.

The Lemon Curd Needs Stirring Immediately After the pressure has released, don't skip the step of stirring the curd. Do it while they are still in the pressure cooker as that saves you having to touch red-hot jars. It is really important because, if you don't, the curd will separate.

KILNER

POULTRY & MEAT

HOW LONG TO COOK A WHOLE CHICKEN IN THE PRESSURE COOKER?

Pressure cooking a whole chicken is delicious. It's similar to slow cooking poultry where the meat falls off the bone. It is so juicy and you just have to have more. It's perfect as a roast dinner but leftovers can be used in any recipe that calls for shredded chicken. You can also use the leftover meat for chicken pies, stews, meal prep and so much more.

But it all starts with the pressure cooker process – in other words, how the chicken cooks in the pressure cooker and, most importantly, how long to cook it.

What I find most fascinating is the fact that there is a simple calculation for working out how long to cook your chicken in the pressure cooker. This will be your cooking time best friend because we don't all buy chickens of the exact same size – yours might be medium, large, extra-large, or even an in-between size. Simply use our calculation and you'll know exactly how long to cook your first pressure cooker chicken.

ROSEMARY & THYME WHOLE CHICKEN

SERVES 4

PREP 5 MINS

SAUTE 0 MINS

PRESSURE COOK 24 MINS

RELEASE DR

TOTAL COOK TIME 24 MINS

399 CALS

2 tsp extra virgin olive oil
1.8kg/4lb whole chicken
2 tsp dried rosemary
2 tsp dried thyme
240ml/8½fl oz/1 cup cold chicken stock

01 Drizzle the olive oil all over the chicken. Add a generous seasoning of salt and pepper, then sprinkle over the rosemary and thyme. Use your hands to coat the chicken.

02 Pour the chicken stock into the cooking pot. Add the trivet/rack, then place the whole chicken, breast side up, on the trivet.

03 Secure the pressure cooker lid and set the valve to sealing. Pressure cook for 24 minutes (6 minutes per 450g/1lb) plus a 15-minute delayed release.

04 Open the lid, remove the chicken and set it aside to rest for 5 minutes before serving.

POULTRY COOKING TIMES

All the cooking times below require a 5-minute delayed pressure release. The food needs to be placed on the trivet/rack with 240ml/8½fl oz/1 cup cold liquid in the cooking pot.

Small chicken breasts 4 mins

Medium chicken breasts 8 mins

Large chicken breasts 15 mins

Chicken thighs, bone in 25 mins

Whole duck (2.5kg/5lb 8oz) 35 mins

Before serving don't forget to take an internal temp, as chicken needs to be 70°C/165°F or above.

WHOLE CHICKEN FOR THE FREEZER

We often have whole chickens in our freezer. They help to cut the cost of groceries, as we buy them when they're on offer and freeze them for another day. I keep them in heavy-duty freezer bags and label them.

You have two main options for pressure cooking: either thaw the chicken (we get ours out the night before to defrost in the fridge) and follow the cooking times opposite; or cook from frozen (see page 53).

CALCULATING THE WHOLE CHICKEN COOKING TIME

The formula for cooking a whole chicken is 6 minutes per 450g/1lb, rounding it off to the nearest minute where necessary, plus a 15-minute delayed release. Let me share some examples:

A I picked up a 1.78kg chicken from the supermarket. Since 1.8kg is 4lbs, I rounded it up slightly. For each 1lb I need to cook for 6 minutes, so I multiplied 6 by 4, which makes 24 minutes cooking time. I then added a 15-minute delayed pressure release. (You could also have worked this out by dividing 1.78kg, or 1780 grams, by 450g. This makes 3.95 – multiply this by 6 for the number of minutes.)

B I picked up a much bigger chicken, one that was 2.8kg/6lb 3oz. As the pound weight isn't a neat number, it is easiest to work it out in grams. Divide 2.8kg or 2800g by 450 to get 6.2. Multiply 6 minutes by 6.2 and you get 37.2 minutes. Round it off to the nearest minute (37), then add your 15-minute delayed release. (Once you've worked it out, you can see it makes sense with the pound quantity, too – 6lb 3oz is 6.2lb!)

Once you've worked out the exact cooking time for your particular size of chicken, then you're ready to pressure cook.

SERVES 4

PREP 2 MINS

SAUTE 0 MINS

PRESSURE COOK 36 MINS

RELEASE DR

TOTAL COOK TIME 36 MINS

399 CALS

COOK FROM FROZEN WHOLE CHICKEN

This recipe is dedicated to all those times when your dinner plans changed at the last minute, or when you forgot to take something out of the freezer. It is actually possible to cook a whole chicken for dinner from frozen!

240ml/8½fl oz/1 cup cold chicken stock
1.8kg/4lb frozen whole chicken
2 tsp dried thyme

01 Pour the chicken stock into the cooking pot and add the trivet/rack. Place the whole chicken, breast side down, onto the trivet.

02 Secure the pressure cooker lid and set the valve to sealing. Pressure cook for 36 minutes, followed by a 5-minute delayed release.

03 Open the lid, remove the chicken, flip it over and season it with salt, pepper and the thyme before serving.

Internal Temperature When cooking poultry, remember to take an internal temperature in the thickest part and make sure it reaches 70°C/165°F or above.

FROZEN POULTRY & MEAT COOKING TIMES

All these cooking times require a 5-minute delayed pressure release. The food needs to be placed on the trivet/rack with 240ml/8½fl oz/1 cup cold liquid in the cooking pot. The food comes out just as moist as when it is cooked from chilled, from the fridge or thawed; it just requires a slightly longer cooking time. It's best to season afterwards and not before.

450g/1lb frozen poussin 22 mins

900g/2lb frozen pork tenderloin 45 mins

1.5kg/3lb 5oz frozen pork loin 70 mins

Frozen pork chops 6 mins

1.3kg/3lb frozen beef roasting joint 1hr 10mins

Frozen lamb chops 3 mins

Frozen bone-in skin-on chicken thighs 16 mins

SERVES
2

PREP
5 MINS

SAUTE
7 MINS

PRESSURE COOK
15 MINS

RELEASE
DR

TOTAL COOK TIME
22 MINS

639 CALS

BUTTER, WINE & PARMESAN POUSSINS

Poussins - often called baby chickens or, as I know them, Cornish game hens - are much smaller than your standard chicken, but are flavoursome and, because of their size, you can easily fit two in the pressure cooker at once.

1 tbsp extra virgin olive oil
2 poussins/Cornish game hens (450g/1lb each), legs tied
240ml/8½fl oz/1 cup dry white wine
2 tsp fresh thyme leaves
4 garlic cloves
2 tsp salted butter
1 x 150g/5½oz pack garlic and herb cream cheese (we use Boursin)
28g/1oz/⅓ cup grated Parmesan
2 tsp roughly chopped fresh parsley

01 Press sauté. Drizzle the olive oil into the cooking pot and, as it warms up, add the poussins and sear the skin to give it a nice crispness.

02 Press cancel, remove the poussins and deglaze the pot with the white wine. Season the birds with salt and pepper, and sprinkle over fresh thyme.

03 Peel the garlic cloves and chop them into medium slices. Add them to the pot, then place the trivet/rack inside. Arrange the poussins on the trivet, breast side up.

04 Secure the pressure cooker lid and set the valve to sealing. Pressure cook for 15 minutes, followed by a 5-minute delayed release.

05 Open the lid, remove the trivet and set aside the poussins.

06 Press sauté, then add the butter and two cheeses to the pot. Mix with the cooking juices to create a sauce. Leave to sauté for a couple of minutes, then press cancel and stir in the parsley. Serve the poussins with the white wine sauce and perhaps some broccolini and carrot and swede mash (see page 150) alongside.

Feeding Just One You can cook just one poussin, if you prefer. Keep the rest of the ingredients the same.

Chicken & Cheese Spread If there is any leftover sauce, place it in a little dish and chill in the fridge. It will then become a delicious garlic-butter-style spread. Have it on toast, or use it to make croutons with your next soup.

TRIVET CHICKEN BREASTS

SERVES
4

PREP
3 MINS

SAUTE
0 MINS

PRESSURE COOK
10 MINS

RELEASE
DR

TOTAL COOK TIME
10 MINS

324 CALS

This is a great trick for the perfect juicy chicken – pressure cooking the chicken breasts above the liquid on the trivet/rack. Plus, it's easy to mix and match with your favourite seasonings or dried mixed herbs.

- 240ml/8½fl oz/1 cup cold chicken stock
- 4 large skinless and boneless chicken breasts (300g/10½oz each)
- 1 tsp extra virgin olive oil
- Pinch of garlic powder
- 1 tsp dried oregano
- 1 tsp dried mixed herbs

01 Pour the chicken stock into the cooking pot and add the trivet/rack.

02 Arrange the chicken breasts on the trivet, spreading them out so that they don't overlap. Drizzle the olive oil over the top, then sprinkle with the herbs, including a generous amount of salt and pepper.

03 Secure the pressure cooker lid and set the valve to sealing. Pressure cook for 10 minutes, followed by a 5-minute delayed release.

04 Open the lid and lift out the trivet and the chicken breasts. Slice the chicken to serve.

FROZEN CURRIED CHICKEN BREASTS

SERVES
4

PREP
2 MINS

SAUTE
0 MINS

PRESSURE COOK
20 MINS

RELEASE
DR

TOTAL COOK TIME
20 MINS

549 CALS

Forgotten to defrost the chicken for dinner? This quick method is your emergency back-up plan – one frozen curry sauce cube defrosted and some frozen chicken.

- 4 medium frozen skinless and boneless chicken breasts (approximately 250g/9oz each)
- 1 × 250ml/9fl oz/1 cup frozen hidden veg curry sauce cube, defrosted (see page 137)

01 Pour 240ml/8½fl oz/1 cup cold water into the cooking pot. Add a teaspoon of the curry sauce and mix it into the water. Add the chicken breasts to the liquid, spreading them out so that they don't overlap. They should be slightly submerged in the seasoned water.

02 Pour the remaining curry sauce over the chicken but don't stir it in. You want to cover the chicken completely.

03 Secure the pressure cooker lid and set the valve to sealing. Pressure cook for 20 minutes, followed by a 5-minute delayed release.

04 Open the lid and use a fork to remove the chicken breasts. Slice the chicken before serving. They will be very tender and you'll never believe they were cooked from frozen.

LEMON PEPPER SHREDDED CHICKEN

SERVES 4

PREP 2 MINS

SAUTE 0 MINS

PRESSURE COOK 8 MINS

RELEASE DR

TOTAL COOK TIME 8 MINS

318 CALS

- 4 large skinless and boneless chicken breasts (approximately 300g/10½oz each)
- 5 tsp lemon pepper seasoning

Shredded chicken and the pressure cooker are a match made in food heaven. You'll be surprised how tender and juicy it is, and how well it falls apart. The chicken cooks in the liquid, which helps keep it moist. You can use it for meal prep, dips, to add to recipes and so much more.

01 Pour 480ml/17fl oz/2 cups cold water into the cooking pot. Add 4 teaspoons of the lemon pepper seasoning and mix it into the water. Add the chicken breasts, spreading them out so that they don't overlap. They should be partly submerged in the seasoned water.

02 Secure the pressure cooker lid and set the valve to sealing. Pressure cook for 8 minutes, followed by a 5-minute delayed release.

03 Open the lid and use a fork to remove the chicken breasts. Shred the chicken with meat claws or a knife and fork, then season with salt and pepper and the remaining lemon pepper seasoning. It's now ready to serve.

Flavour It Up You can use any seasoning for your shredded chicken – try coconut lime, Caribbean curry powder, taco seasoning, fajita seasoning or any other dried seasoning.

Talking About Fajitas If you head to page 166, you'll spot our chicken fajitas recipe. This follows the shredding method but takes it to the next level by cooking the onion and peppers at the same time.

Freezer Friendly Chicken You could shred the chicken, let it cool, then transfer it to freezer bags. It will keep for up to 3 days in the fridge or 3 months in the freezer. It is also brilliant for sandwiches and adding to soups and casseroles.

PARTY NIGHT SPICY CHICKEN THIGHS

SERVES
4

PREP
5 MINS

SAUTE
4 MINS

PRESSURE COOK
4 MINS

RELEASE
DR

TOTAL COOK TIME
8 MINS

525 CALS

- 3 tbsp hot sauce (we use Nando's peri peri medium sauce)
- 1 tbsp salted butter, melted
- 1 tbsp brown sugar
- 1 tbsp soy sauce
- 2 tbsp barbecue sauce
- 1 tsp each garlic powder, sweet paprika and dried parsley
- 1.3kg/3lb boneless and skinless chicken thighs
- 1 × 165g/5¾oz pack full-fat cream cheese (we use Philadelphia)

I love this spicy chicken recipe for party nights. The leftovers taste amazing in tortilla wraps the next day, too.

01 Pour 120ml/4fl oz/½ cup cold water into the cooking pot. Add ½ teaspoon of the hot sauce and mix it into the water.

02 Place the remaining hot sauce, the melted butter, sugar, soy sauce, barbecue sauce and the seasonings in a bowl. Stir everything together, then add the chicken and mix well with your hands.

03 Place the seasoned chicken thighs in the seasoned water. They will be slightly submerged. Pour any bits of marinade left in the bowl over the chicken.

04 Secure the pressure cooker lid and set the valve to sealing. Pressure cook for 4 minutes, followed by a 3-minute delayed release.

05 Open the lid and use a fork to remove the chicken thighs. Shred the chicken with meat claws or a knife and fork. Season with salt and pepper.

06 Keep just 240ml/8½fl oz/1 cup of the cooking liquid in the pot, press sauté, and stir in the cream cheese. Sauté with a wooden spoon until you have a creamy sauce. Let it bubble away and reduce a little. Do a taste test, and if it's not spicy enough, add a little more hot sauce. Remember to be patient and add a tiny bit at a time, as you don't want it to be overly spicy.

07 Cancel sauté, add the shredded chicken and stir. It's now ready to serve.

Hot Sauce Any hot sauce you have will work in this recipe. I also love to switch it up and use red-hot sauce or sriracha.

SERVES
4

PREP
5 MINS

SAUTE
5 MINS

PRESSURE COOK
5 MINS

RELEASE
QPR

TOTAL COOK TIME
10 MINS

829 CALS

10-MINUTE TERIYAKI CHICKEN NOODLES

After showing you two different ways to cook shredded chicken in the pressure cooker, one using chicken breasts and one with boneless chicken thighs, we wanted to show you how to make it into a favourite dinner. Shredded chicken, fresh egg noodles, teriyaki sauce and green beans - what more could you possibly want?

- 1.3kg/3lb skinless and boneless chicken thighs
- 2 tsp Chinese five spice
- 1 medium red onion
- 240ml/8½fl oz/1 cup teriyaki sauce (we use Blue Dragon)
- 1 tbsp plain/all-purpose flour
- 1 tbsp soy sauce
- 2 tbsp runny honey
- 1 tsp garlic purée
- 1 tsp ginger purée
- 600g/1lb 5oz fresh egg noodles
- 100g/3½oz frozen green beans
- Roughly chopped fresh coriander/cilantro, to serve
- Lime wedges, to serve

01 Pour 120ml/4fl oz/½ cup cold water into the cooking pot. Add a teaspoon of the Chinese five spice and stir into the water. This is your stock. Add the chicken thighs so they are partly submerged. Peel and slice the red onion into strips and add these around the chicken. Pour a quarter of the teriyaki sauce over the chicken to coat them. Don't stir it in.

02 Secure the pressure cooker lid and set the valve to sealing. Pressure cook for 5 minutes, followed by a quick pressure release.

03 Open the lid and use a fork to remove the chicken thighs. Shred the chicken with meat claws or a knife and fork, then season with salt and pepper and the remaining Chinese five spice.

04 Press sauté and, whilst the pot heats up, mix the flour and 3 tablespoons water together in a small bowl to make a thick, creamy paste.

05 Stir the flour paste into the cooking liquid, as it will thicken the sauce. Add the remaining teriyaki sauce, the soy sauce, honey and purées, then give it all a really good stir.

06 Finally, add the egg noodles and green beans and continue to stir. The green beans will warm through quickly from frozen. Press cancel, then return the shredded chicken to the pot, season again with salt and pepper, and give it one last stir before serving with fresh coriander and lime wedges.

Switch the Sauce We use a deliciously thick teriyaki sauce, but you could swap it for another favourite. Try it with sweet chilli, oyster or black bean sauce.

CHRISTMAS GAMMON

SERVES 8

PREP 15 MINS

SAUTE 0 MINS

PRESSURE COOK 45 MINS

RELEASE DR

TOTAL COOK TIME 45 MINS

535 CALS

- 4 Pink Lady apples
- 4 pears
- 1 × 440ml/16fl oz can apple or pear (hard) cider
- 1.8kg/4lb gammon/ham joint
- 1 garlic bulb
- 2 heaped tbsp granulated sugar
- 1 tsp ground cinnamon
- ¼ tsp mixed spice/apple spice

Gammon (uncooked ham to our friends across the pond) is my go-to at Christmas time. We could only get a small gammon when we lived in Portugal, except for at Christmas time, so we really looked forward to it. As gammon can be salty, you can use the pressure cooker to reduce the salt levels, and also make your apple and pear cider sauce at the same time!

01 Peel and remove the cores of the apples and pears. Chop them into chunks and add to the cooking pot.

02 If the gammon has netting, use a knife to remove it. If you don't like fat, you can trim any excess. Peel the garlic cloves and insert them into the scores in the fat.

03 Place the gammon over the apples and pears in the cooking pot. Pour in the cider.

04 Secure the pressure cooker lid and set the valve to sealing. Pressure cook for 45 minutes, followed by a 5-minute delayed pressure release.

05 Remove the gammon with a fork, cover with foil and set aside to rest for 5 minutes.

06 Meanwhile, drain the liquid from the cooking pot, reserving the apple and pear chunks. Sprinkle in the sugar, cinnamon and mixed spice. Give everything a stir, then serve the fruity sauce with the gammon. (The apple and pear sauce also tastes delicious in sandwiches with any leftover gammon.)

Want an Alcohol-free Recipe? Swap the (hard) cider for the same quantity of apple or pear juice.

Fizzy Drinks Option You could also swap the cider for cola, Fanta or lemonade.

STAND UP PORK RIBS

SERVES 4

PREP 5 MINS

SAUTE 0 MINS

PRESSURE COOK 30 MINS

RELEASE DR

TOTAL COOK TIME 30 MINS

490 CALS

We had always cooked our pork ribs in the slow cooker for 7 hours on low. It was easy - you simply added them in with the marinade, slow cooked and then had tasty ribs in the evening. But then I got a pressure cooker and we realised we could do them in less than an hour, including the time to pressure. There is also a hack that is possible with a pressure cooker but not with a slow cooker, because of the depth of the cooking pot - ribs can be positioned around the cooking pot standing upright, which makes them ridiculously tender, too.

- 240ml/9fl oz/1 cup cold chicken stock
- 1 × 440ml/16fl oz can sweet (hard) apple cider
- 1 tbsp Worcestershire sauce
- 900g/2lb pork ribs (we use 2 × 450g/1lb racks)

BARBECUE OYSTER SAUCE

- 4 tbsp oyster sauce (we use Blue Dragon)
- 3 tbsp runny honey
- 2 tsp barbecue sauce (we use Bull's-Eye)
- 1 tsp tomato ketchup
- 1 tsp ginger purée
- 1 tsp garlic purée
- 1 tsp soft brown sugar

01 Pour the stock, cider and Worcestershire sauce into the cooking pot.

02 Add the ribs and arrange them upright in a circle, leaning them against the sides of the cooking pot. Create a second circle inside the first with any remaining ribs. They should be three-quarters submerged in the stock.

03 Secure the pressure cooker lid and set the valve to sealing. Pressure cook for 30 minutes, followed by a 5-minute delayed release.

04 Open the lid and carefully use tongs to remove the ribs. Transfer them to a tray large enough to hold them all. (Remember these ribs are very tender, so be careful as you remove them.) Season the ribs with salt and black pepper.

05 Mix the sauce ingredients together in a small bowl, then use a pastry brush to cover the ribs in the sticky oyster glaze. Serve with baby wipes nearby.

Want an Alcohol-free Recipe? Swap the (hard) cider for the same quantity of apple or pear juice.

2 Racks or 4? Because the racks wind round the edges of the cooking pot, it's easy to increase to 3 or 4 racks of ribs. If you fancy 4 racks instead of 2, double the pork and barbecue oyster sauce but keep the other pork ingredients the same.

Go Korean Over the page we have Korean-inspired pulled pork sauce. You could use that sauce in this recipe instead and make Korean barbecue ribs.

Just Grab a Different Bottle Prefer black bean, plum sauce, or hoisin? Substitute the oyster sauce for any of these to add a different flavour to your sauce.

Love Pork Belly Add pork belly slices instead of standing ribs. The cooking time is much quicker, at 15 minutes.

BARBECUE PULLED PORK SANDWICHES (2 WAYS)

SERVES 6

PREP 10 MINS

SAUTE 0 MINS

PRESSURE COOK 1 HR

RELEASE NPR

TOTAL COOK TIME 1 HR

525 CALS CLASSIC
548 CALS KOREAN-STYLE

1.3kg/3lb boneless pork shoulder, trimmed of fat
360ml/12fl oz/1½ cups apple juice or (hard) apple cider
120ml/4fl oz/½ cup barbecue sauce
6 brioche buns
Finely grated carrot, spring/green onion, red cabbage and fresh coriander/cilantro, to serve

CLASSIC BBQ PORK (OPTION 1)

2 tbsp soft brown sugar
1 tbsp smoked paprika
2 tsp ground cumin
1 tsp garlic powder
4 tbsp tomato ketchup
1 tbsp Dijon mustard
1 tbsp Worcestershire sauce

KOREAN-STYLE BBQ PORK (OPTION 2)

2 tbsp ginger purée
2 tbsp garlic purée
1 tbsp soy sauce
2 tbsp rice wine vinegar
100g/3½oz/½ cup soft brown sugar
1 tsp chilli flakes
3 tbsp runny honey
2 tbsp tomato ketchup
½ jar pickled red jalapeños, blended until smooth (adjust to taste – see jar tip below)

Slow cooking pulled pork takes about 4 hours, but pressure cooker pulled pork is done in 1 hour! This pulled pork is so good, I can guarantee you'll want seconds. We've made 2 delicious versions – a classic barbecue and a Korean-style barbecue.

01 Choose one of the two pork sauces, then place all of the sauce ingredients in a large mixing bowl. Stir until well combined. Set aside half of the sauce in a jug, then add the pork to the bowl with the remaining sauce and turn it over a few times to get it fully coated. Cover the bowl with cling film/plastic wrap and leave to marinate in the fridge for at least 2 hours, but overnight is even better.

02 Remove the marinated pork from the bowl and place it in the cooking pot. Pour the apple juice or cider into the bowl and stir well so any residual sauce is mixed into the juice. Pour this into the cooking pot over the pork.

03 Secure the pressure cooker lid and set the valve to sealing. Pressure cook for 1 hour, followed by a full natural pressure release.

04 Open the lid and use a fork to remove the pork. Set aside to rest in a large bowl. When it's cool enough to handle, use meat claws or a knife and fork to shred the pork.

05 Add the barbecue sauce to the bowl with the pork, as well as the reserved jug of sauce. Season generously with salt and pepper, and mix everything together with a fork. Serve the pulled pork in a brioche bun with sliced red cabbage, finely grated carrot, spring onions, fresh coriander and some crisps/potato chips.

A Jar of Pickled Jalapeños Whether green or red jalapeños, they help make an incredible base for a sauce. Simply blend a full jar of pickled jalapeños – including the liquid – then pour them back into the jar and store in the fridge. Use them in this Korean-inspired pulled pork and other similar recipes.

SERVES
6

PREP
15 MINS

SAUTE
8 MINS

PRESSURE COOK
51 MINS

RELEASE
NPR/QR

TOTAL COOK TIME
59 MINS

405 CALS

- 1.3kg/3lb beef braising joint/chuck roast
- 1 tbsp extra virgin olive oil
- 1 medium brown onion
- 1 garlic bulb
- 4 celery sticks
- 2 tbsp salted butter
- 960ml/32½fl oz/4 cups cold beef stock
- 900g/2lb baby potatoes, scrubbed
- 450g/1lb Chantenay carrots/baby carrots, scrubbed
- 2 tbsp Worcestershire sauce
- 2 tsp dried thyme
- 1 tbsp finely chopped fresh parsley
- 1 tbsp tomato purée/paste
- 1 tbsp gravy granules

BEEF POT ROAST

My favourite American one pot is simplified here using the pressure cooker. Firstly, we cook the amazing braising joint/chuck roast, then whilst it rests, we cook the fork-tender potatoes and carrots. To finish, we make a rich gravy from the cooking juices in the pot.

01 Chop the beef into 3–4 medium chunks. Place them in the cooking pot, drizzle with the olive oil, then press sauté and brown on all sides. Remove the beef with tongs and set aside.

02 Peel and slice the onion into chunks, peel the garlic cloves and cut them into thin slices, clean the celery sticks and cut them into medium slices. Add all of the prepared veg to the cooking pot, then add 1 tablespoon of the butter and continue sautéing until the onion has softened. Press cancel.

03 Return the meat to the pot and pour in the beef stock.

04 Secure the pressure cooker lid and set the valve to sealing. Pressure cook for 45 minutes, followed by a full natural pressure release.

05 Open the lid and remove the beef, setting it to one side. (The beef will be pull apart, so you may find it easier to remove it with a ladle.)

06 Place the baby potatoes in the cooking pot (if they are big, slice them in half) and add the carrots. Secure the pressure cooker lid for a second time and set the valve to sealing. Pressure cook for 6 minutes, followed by a quick pressure release.

07 In the meantime, shred the beef with meat claws or a knife and fork. Drizzle with the Worcestershire sauce, and season generously with salt and pepper and the dried thyme.

08 Arrange the shredded meat, potatoes and carrots on a large platter. Season the potatoes and carrots with salt and pepper, and sprinkle with fresh parsley. Dot the veg with the remaining butter, so it melts into them.

09 Place the tomato purée and gravy granules in the cooking pot with the juices, onion, garlic and celery. Blend with a stick blender, then stir to make a rich gravy. Pour over the beef and serve.

Extra Gravy As we're making use of all the liquid in the pot, this will be enough gravy for at least two meals. Once cold, freeze any leftovers for another pressure cooker dinner.

Pulled Beef If you're just craving some pulled beef, you can make it by following steps 1 to 5. Use meat claws to shred. You could then add a sauce of choice, depending how you are serving it – try the Korean-style sauce from page 67 or keep it basic with gravy for a leftover beef soup or beef pie.

SERVES
8

PREP
10 MINS

SAUTE
8 MINS

PRESSURE COOK
20 MINS

RELEASE
DR

TOTAL COOK TIME
28 MINS

283 CALS

LEFTOVER BEEF & BARLEY SOUP

After making the beef pot roast (from page 69), I usually have a bit of beef left over. It's times like these when I make a big batch of beef soup. This is a truly hearty soup, it serves the whole family for dinner, and there's plenty left over for the freezer, too.

- 1 medium brown onion
- 4 large carrots
- 4 celery sticks
- 1 tbsp extra virgin olive oil
- 240ml/8½fl oz/1 cup red wine
- 1.2l/40fl oz/5 cups cold beef stock
- 225g/8oz baby potatoes, scrubbed and quartered
- 200g/7oz/1 cup pearl barley
- 250g/9oz leftover pulled beef (see page 69)
- 500g/1lb 2oz/2 cups passata
- 160g/5¾oz/1 cup frozen peas
- 1 tbsp celery salt
- 2 tsp dried thyme
- 2 tsp dried rosemary
- 1 tsp garlic powder
- 2 tsp sweet paprika

01 Peel and chop the onion and carrots. Clean and chop the celery. Add the olive oil and prepared veg to the pot and sauté until the onion has softened. Press cancel.

02 Deglaze the pot with the red wine, then pour in the beef stock. Add the potatoes and pearl barley, and stir.

03 Secure the pressure cooker lid and set the valve to sealing. Pressure cook for 20 minutes, followed by a 5-minute delayed release.

04 If you're planning to eat the soup straigt away, stir in the beef, passata, frozen peas and all the remaining ingredients, along with a generous seasoning of salt and pepper, and use the residual heat from the cooking pot to warm everything through. It's now ready to serve. (It's only safe to reheat once, so you don't want to add the beef, then freeze it and reheat again at another time.)

Using Raw Beef? This recipe is based on cooked beef. But if you want to make this with raw beef, then start by sautéing the beef. Follow the same method, just increase the pressure cooker time to 45 minutes.

Skip a Bit of Prep On page 139 we show you how to make mirepoix cubes for the freezer, which are made up of onion, celery, carrots and stock. Grab one of those from the freezer and defrost it here, as it will save you some time.

SERVES
4

PREP
8 MINS

SAUTE
8 MINS

PRESSURE COOK
48 MINS

RELEASE
DR/QPR

TOTAL COOK TIME
56 MINS

624 CALS

1.3kg/3lb bone-in leg of lamb
1 tbsp extra virgin olive oil
4 garlic cloves
225g/8oz butternut squash, peeled and roughly chopped (prepared weight)
1 × 400g/14oz can coconut milk
500g/1lb 2oz/2 cups passata
¼ tsp cayenne pepper (adjust to taste)
1 tbsp roughly chopped fresh coriander/cilantro

CURRY SPICE BLEND

1 tbsp ground cumin
2 tbsp garam masala
1½ tsp ground coriander
1 tsp garlic powder
½ tsp turmeric

LEG OF LAMB CURRY

Transform your leg of lamb into a delicious lamb curry. Loaded with pressure-cooked butternut squash and served with mushroom rice (see page 174), this is a real feast. We also love to serve this with the saag aloo (see page 155).

01 Pat the lamb dry with kitchen/paper towel. Score the lamb (this will help the flavours penetrate the lamb). Mix the curry spice blend ingredients in a small bowl.

02 Drizzle the olive oil over the lamb, then sprinkle over a tablespoon of the spice blend. Use your hands to rub the spices into the lamb.

03 Pour 240ml/8½fl oz/1 cup cold water into the cooking pot, then add a teaspoon of the spice blend to the water and stir. Place the trivet/rack in the pot, then arrange the leg of lamb on top.

04 Secure the pressure cooker lid and set the valve to sealing. Pressure cook for 45 minutes, followed by a 5-minute delayed release.

05 Open the lid and remove the trivet and the lamb. Cover with foil and set it aside to rest. Meanwhile, peel and thinly slice the garlic and add this to the cooking pot along with the prepared butternut squash. Secure the pressure cooker lid and set the valve to sealing. Pressure cook for 3 minutes, followed by a quick pressure release.

06 Remove the bone from the lamb, then chop the meat into chunks.

07 Drain the liquid from the cooking pot. Pour in the coconut milk and passata. Press sauté and stir in the remaining spice blend and the cayenne pepper, adjusting to taste. Stir in the lamb chunks, then let it bubble away for a couple of minutes to reduce. Press cancel.

08 Serve the lamb curry with mushroom rice (see page 174) and saag aloo (see page 155) for the ultimate fakeaway.

SERVES 4
PREP 2 MINS
SAUTE 0 MINS
PRESSURE COOK 2 MINS
RELEASE DR
TOTAL COOK TIME 2 MINS

281 CALS

DEFROSTING MINCED BEEF

You want mince for dinner but it's frozen? This is an easy method for a quick defrost.

500g/1lb 2oz frozen minced/ground beef

01 Pour 240ml/8½fl oz/1 cup cold water into the cooking pot. Add the trivet/rack and place the block of frozen minced beef on top. (The cooking time is calculated to work perfectly with one large, thick block of mince – it won't work as well if you have smaller blocks.)

02 Secure the pressure cooker lid and set the valve to sealing. Pressure cook for 2 minutes, followed by a 5-minute delayed release.

03 Your mince will be browned around the edges and totally defrosted in the centre – perfect and ready to cook (see below and page 183 for great ways to cook mince).

Mix & Match Swap minced/ground beef for frozen minced pork, chicken, turkey, lamb or veal.

SERVES 4
PREP 3 MINS
SAUTE 5 MINS
PRESSURE COOK 0 MINS
RELEASE N/A
TOTAL COOK TIME 5 MINS

290 CALS

EMERGENCY TACO MEAT

I've shown you how to defrost mince, now here's one way to use it after defrosting. Introducing you to delicious taco meat – perfect for your next taco Tuesday.

500g/1lb 2oz minced/ground beef (defrosted as above, if frozen)
2 tbsp taco seasoning
2 tbsp salsa dip

01 Press sauté, and add the mince to the empty cooking pot. Use a wooden spoon to break down the block of mince as you sauté. Sprinkle in the taco seasoning and a generous seasoning of salt and pepper.

02 When the mince is almost cooked through, stir in the salsa, then continue to sauté until fully cooked. Press cancel.

03 Serve with all your favourite taco garnishes.

Mix & Match Swap the taco seasoning and salsa for some mixed Italian herbs and pasta sauce to transform this into a Bolognese-style dish instead.

Make Your Own Taco Seasoning Combine 1 teaspoon each of sea salt, garlic and onion powder, 2 teaspoons each of dried oregano, smoked paprika and ground cumin, and ¼ teaspoon each of cayenne powder and freshly ground black pepper in an air-tight container or herb jar. Cover with a lid and give it a shake. It will keep in your pantry for 6 months.

DIRTY WATER DOGS

SERVES 4

PREP 5 MINS

SAUTE 5 MINS

PRESSURE COOK 0 MINS

RELEASE QPR

TOTAL COOK TIME 5 MINS

303 CALS

1 medium brown onion
1 tbsp extra virgin olive oil
1 tsp balsamic vinegar
1 tsp apple cider vinegar
½ tsp ground cumin
Pinch of ground nutmeg
4 bratwurst or frankfurter sausages
4 hotdog buns

This is the name given to New York-style hotdogs. You cook the hotdogs in water that is flavoured to replicate the water used by New York hotdog stands.

01 Press sauté. Peel and slice the onion, then add it to the cooking pot with the olive oil. Sauté until the onions are beautifully soft and have started to brown. Press cancel, remove the onions from the pot and set aside. (If you don't want to serve onions with your hotdogs, you can skip this step.)

02 Pour 480ml/17fl oz/2 cups cold water into the cooking pot. Add both vinegars and the cumin and nutmeg, and stir. This is the dirty water! Add the sausages, spreading them out so that they don't overlap.

03 Secure the pressure cooker lid and set the valve to sealing. Pressure cook for 0 minutes, followed by a quick pressure release.

04 Remove the hotdogs with tongs, place them in the buns and top with the sautéed onions. Squirt some ketchup and mustard over them, too, if you like.

Brats Otherwise known as bratwurst, brats are the best sausages to use in the pressure cooker. Other kinds of sausage can pop open from the pressure.

FOIL PACKET BURGERS

SERVES 4

PREP 2 MINS

SAUTE 0 MINS

PRESSURE COOK 20 MINS

RELEASE QPR

TOTAL COOK TIME 20 MINS

437 CALS

4 frozen lean beef quarter pounders
4 burger buns

Another last-minute dinner, here's a great burger hack – a recipe for pressure cooking frozen burgers. Just choose your garnish, whether that's lettuce, tomatoes or gherkins, etc.

01 Pour 240ml/8½fl oz/1 cup cold water into the cooking pot and add the trivet/rack. Wrap each burger individually in foil and place them on the trivet.

02 Secure the pressure cooker lid and set the valve to sealing. Pressure cook for 20 minutes, followed by a quick pressure release.

03 Unwrap the foil packets and place the burgers in the buns. Top with your favourite garnish and sauce.

Mix & Match Swap the beef burgers for pork or veggie burgers. Chicken burgers go dry if cooked this way, so avoid them.

FISH & SEAFOOD

HOW TO PRESSURE COOK ANY FISH FILLET

In the Milner house we love cooking a fish fillet in the pressure cooker. We still remember the first time (about 10 years ago now) when we cooked our first salmon fillet under pressure. The moment the fork touched the salmon and we saw how it flaked, and there was no going back.

What pressure cooking fish fillets does is similar to steaming. It's just faster. You can even cook fish, like salmon, from frozen in just 4 minutes using the pressure cooker function.

FISH IN THE COOKING POT VERSUS ON THE TRIVET/RACK VERSUS FOIL

There are three main cooking methods with a pressure cooker. Cooking food directly in liquid in the cooking pot, so it's like poaching, having the food out of the liquid on a trivet/rack, or wrapping the food in foil parcels. We would only recommend cooking in the liquid with fish if you are planning to mash the fish afterwards, such as when you're making fish cakes. That leaves trivet versus foil. We like both and the only real difference is that wrapping the fish in foil is going to take slightly longer. However, it's a good method to use if you're planning to cook other things at the same time. So, for example, if you've coated the fish in a sauce and you don't want it leaking out onto other ingredients in the pot, wrapping it in a foil parcel would be a good idea.

PRESSURE COOKER SALMON

SERVES 2

PREP 3 MINS

SAUTE 0 MINS

PRESSURE COOK 2–4 MINS

RELEASE DR

TOTAL COOK TIME 2–4 MINS

250 CALS

2 × 115g/4oz salmon fillets, skin on
2 tsp fish seasoning (see opposite)
1 small lemon
2 tsp salted butter

You can follow the method below with other fish, too. Why not try tilapia, cod, haddock, mackerel, seabass, pollock, basa or seabream.

01 Pour 240ml/8½fl oz/1 cup cold water into the cooking pot and add the trivet/rack.

02 Place a layer of foil on your worktop and arrange the salmon fillets side by side on top. Sprinkle the salmon with the seasoning.

03 Cut the lemon into medium slices. Squeeze a slice of lemon over each fillet, then add 2 slices of lemon to the salmon. Place a teaspoonful of butter on top of each fillet.

04 Now, depending on how you are cooking your salmon, either place the foil flat over the trivet or wrap the foil up around the salmon to create a salmon packet and place on the trivet. Secure the pressure cooker lid and set the valve to sealing. Pressure cook for 4 minutes, followed by a 3-minute delayed release if wrapped in foil. If not wrapped, pressure cook for 2 minutes, followed by a 2-minute delayed release.

05 Open the lid, remove the salmon and serve with the remaining lemon slices.

FISH SEASONING

This seasoning mix is our go-to for everything fish in the pressure cooker. Load all the herbs and spices into a herb jar and store to use later. Look out for recipes in this chapter using this seasoning.

1 tbsp celery salt
1 tbsp smoked paprika
1½ tsp mustard powder
1½ tsp mixed spice/apple pie spice
1 tsp garlic powder
¾ tsp ground black pepper
¾ tsp nutmeg
¼ tsp ground allspice

FISH COOK TIMES

Salmon fillets on the rack 2 mins + 2dr

Salmon fillets wrapped in foil 4 mins + 3dr

Seabass fish fillets wrapped in foil 2 mins + 2dr

Whole tilapia 10 mins + 5dr

Frozen salmon fillets on the rack 4 mins + 2dr

Frozen tuna fillets on the rack 6 mins + 2dr

Frozen cod fillets on the rack 4 mins + 2dr

EMERGENCY TUNA & ASPARAGUS FOR ONE

SERVES 1

PREP 4 MINS

SAUTE 0 MINS

PRESSURE COOK 6 MINS

RELEASE QPR

TOTAL COOK TIME 6 MINS

265 CALS

1 frozen tuna steak (2.5cm/1in thick)
4 asparagus spears
115g/4oz cherry tomatoes
2 tsp balsamic vinegar
1 tsp extra virgin olive oil
2 tsp roughly chopped fresh basil, plus sprigs to serve
1 tsp salted butter
Sprinkle of chilli flakes
Zest of 1 lime

Didn't get anything out of the freezer for dinner? Looking for a quick fix? Then you'll love this. Tuna steaks cooked from frozen with asparagus. And while it cooks, prep some quick cherry tomatoes with a balsamic drizzle.

01 Pour 240ml/8½fl oz/1 cup cold water into the cooking pot and add the trivet/rack. Cover it with foil to stop any food falling through the gaps.

02 Place the tuna and asparagus on the rack. Secure the pressure cooker lid and set the valve to sealing. Pressure cook for 6 minutes, followed by a quick pressure release.

03 Whilst the tuna and asparagus are cooking, cut the cherry tomatoes in half, place in a bowl, drizzle them with balsamic vinegar and olive oil, season them with salt and pepper, and stir in the chopped basil.

04 Open the lid of the pressure cooker and remove the tuna and asparagus. Transfer to the bowl with the cherry tomatoes. Add a little butter to the asparagus, season the tuna and asparagus with salt, pepper and chilli flakes, and squeeze some lime over the tuna, before serving with a few basil leaves scattered over the top.

SERVES
2

PREP
3 MINS

SAUTE
6 MINS

PRESSURE COOK
12 MINS

RELEASE
QPR

TOTAL COOK TIME
18 MINS

484 CALS

PRAWN PIL PIL

Did you know you can pressure cook a whole garlic bulb? Then you can squeeze out the perfectly cooked garlic. No need for peeling and perfect for reducing your prep time. We will first be showing you how to do this and then using the garlic to make delicious prawn pil pil.

- 1 garlic bulb
- 120ml/½ cup extra virgin olive oil
- 250g/9oz raw peeled super king prawns/shrimp
- 2 tsp smoked paprika
- ¼ tsp chilli flakes
- Roughly chopped fresh parsley, to serve
- Squeeze of fresh lemon juice

01 Pour 240ml/8½fl oz/1 cup cold water into the cooking pot and add the trivet/rack.

02 Slice the top off the garlic bulb, exposing the garlic cloves. Drizzle with a teaspoon of the olive oil. Place the garlic on the trivet.

03 Secure the pressure cooker lid and set the valve to sealing. Pressure cook for 12 minutes, followed by a quick pressure release.

04 Open the lid and remove the garlic. Discard the water in the cooking pot.

05 Press sauté and add the prawns and a tablespoon of the olive oil. When the prawns start to go pink, add the paprika, the remaining olive oil and the chilli flakes. Give it a good stir, then press cancel.

06 Squeeze the garlic cloves into the pot (they will be really mushy and squeeze out easily), stir and, once the prawns are cooked, serve in a tapas dish with a sprinkling of parsley, a squeeze of lemon, some crusty bread, marinated olives and aioli.

SERVES 2

PREP 5 MINS

SAUTE 0 MINS

PRESSURE COOK 2 MINS

RELEASE DR

TOTAL COOK TIME 2 MINS

381 CALS

2 x 115g/4oz salmon fillets, skin on
2 tbsp mayonnaise
1 tbsp sweet chilli sauce

SWEET CHILLI MAYO SALMON

This is a delicious hack for perfect salmon in a sauce in the pressure cooker.

01 Pour 240ml/8½fl oz/1 cup cold water into the cooking pot and add the trivet/rack. Place a layer of foil over the trivet, then top with the salmon fillets. Season them with salt and pepper.

02 Mix together the mayonnaise and the sweet chilli sauce, then spoon this mixture over the salmon fillets.

03 Secure the pressure cooker lid and set the valve to sealing. Pressure cook for 2 minutes, followed by a 2-minute delayed release.

04 Open the lid and remove the salmon. Transfer to your plate and serve with brown rice (see page 110).

SERVES 2

PREP 5 MINS

SAUTE 1 MIN

PRESSURE COOK 2 MINS

RELEASE DR

TOTAL COOK TIME 3 MINS

461 CALS

55g/2oz/¼ cup salted butter
360ml/12fl oz/1½ cups dry white wine
4 garlic cloves
800g/1lb 12oz frozen clams
2 tsp roughly chopped fresh parsley

WHITE WINE CLAMS

Frozen clams with white wine, garlic and butter. You just need bread.

01 Press sauté. Add the butter and sauté for about 1 minute until melted. Press cancel.

02 Deglaze the pot with the white wine. Peel and quarter the garlic cloves, then add to the pot with the clams (discard any clams that are already open). Give it a good stir.

03 Secure the pressure cooker lid and set the valve to sealing. Pressure cook for 2 minutes, followed by a 5-minute delayed pressure release.

04 Open the lid, sprinkle with parsley and serve (don't eat any that haven't opened).

SERVES
2

PREP
5 MINS

SAUTE
6 MINS

PRESSURE COOK
2 MINS

RELEASE
DR

TOTAL COOK TIME
8 MINS

765 CALS

- 85g/3oz baby corn
- 85g/3oz mangetout
- 4 × 90g/3¼oz skinless fish fillets (we use seabass, seabream and cod)
- 1 red (bell) pepper/capsicum
- 1 medium red onion
- 1 tbsp extra virgin olive oil
- ½ batch hidden veg curry sauce (see page 137)
- 250g/9oz raw peeled super king prawns/shrimp
- Juice of 1 lime
- ½ tsp ground cumin

MIXED FISH CURRY

This fish curry is healthy yet delicious, with lots of veg hidden in the curry sauce.

01 Pour 240ml/8½fl oz/1 cup cold water into the cooking pot. Add the baby corn and mangetout to the water, then place the trivet/rack over the top. Cover the trivet with foil, then top with the fish fillets.

02 Secure the pressure cooker lid and set the valve to sealing. Pressure cook for 2 minutes, followed by a 2-minute delayed release.

03 Open the lid, discard the liquid and set the veg and fish aside. Chop the fish fillets into thirds.

04 Press sauté and as the pot warms up, deseed and slice the pepper, and peel and dice the onion. Pop them in the cooking pot with the olive oil and sauté for 4 minutes, or until the onion has softened. Stir in the curry sauce and the prawns, and continue to sauté for about 2 minutes, until the prawns are fully cooked.

05 Add the fish and veg back into the pot, squeeze in the lime juice and stir in the cumin. Press cancel and serve.

SERVES
2

PREP
5 MINS

SAUTE
0 MINS

PRESSURE COOK
2 MINS

RELEASE
DR

TOTAL COOK TIME
2 MINS

310 CALS

- 2 × 115g/4oz salmon fillets, skin on
- 6 medium broccoli florets
- 2 tsp extra virgin olive oil
- 2 tsp fish seasoning (see page 79)

2-MINUTE SALMON & BROCCOLI

Because salmon and broccoli have the same cooking time, you can add them to the pot together.

01 Pour 240ml/8½fl oz/1 cup cold water into the cooking pot and add the trivet/rack. Place foil on the trivet, then load it up with the salmon fillets and broccoli. Add a drizzle of olive oil and a sprinkling of salt, pepper and the fish seasoning.

02 Secure the pressure cooker lid and set the valve to sealing. Pressure cook for 2 minutes, followed by a 2-minute delayed release.

03 Open the lid and remove the salmon and broccoli. Divide between two plates and serve.

SERVES
4

PREP
15 MINS

SAUTE
3 MINS

PRESSURE COOK
20 MINS

RELEASE
QPR & DR

TOTAL COOK TIME
23 MINS

681 CALS

MEDITERRANEAN SALMON SALAD & GRAIN BOWL

Did you know that salmon fillets, butternut squash cubes and broccolini have the same cooking time? Here we show you how to make these cooking times work for you. This feeds two and is perfect for a Saturday night fakeaway, though it is also perfect for taking the leftovers to work for lunch on Monday.

200g/7oz/1 cup pearl barley
115g/4oz halloumi, chopped into medium chunks
½ tsp ground cumin
2 pinches of chilli flakes
1 tbsp extra virgin olive oil
8 tenderstem broccoli/broccolini spears, trimmed
115g/4oz butternut squash, cut into 1.5cm/⅝in cubes (prepared weight)
4 x 115g/4oz salmon fillets, skin on
½ lemon
¼ tsp dried dill
4 tbsp hummus (see page 94)

RAINBOW SLAW

1 spring/green onion, thinly sliced
2 radishes, thinly sliced
75g/2¾oz carrot, grated
150g/5½oz red cabbage, thinly shredded
2 tbsp heaped mayonnaise (we use Hellmann's Light)
1 tbsp apple cider vinegar
¼ tsp ground cumin

GRAIN BOWL

¼ tsp ground cumin
¼ tsp fennel seeds
Pinch of ground cinnamon
1 tsp finely chopped dried cranberries
1 tsp sunflower seeds
1 tsp pumpkin seeds

01 Pour 480ml/17fl oz/2 cups cold water into the cooking pot and add the pearl barley. Secure the pressure cooker lid and set the valve to sealing. Pressure cook for 18 minutes, followed by a quick pressure release. (While the pearl barley is cooking, we can prepare the other ingredients.)

02 Let's make the slaw. Add all the ingredients to a bowl and mix well. Set aside.

03 Season the halloumi with the ground cumin and chilli flakes.

04 When the pressure cooker is done, transfer the pearl barley to a medium mixing bowl. Drain any liquid left in the cooking pot, then press sauté. Add the olive oil and halloumi, and toss in the oil. Keep an eye on it, as you don't want the halloumi sticking to the bottom of the pot. As soon as it starts to crisp and has a lovely texture to it, quickly remove the halloumi from the cooking pot and cancel the sauté.

05 Deglaze the pot with 240ml/8½fl oz/1 cup cold water and scrape any bits stuck to the bottom. (It's important you deglaze the pot, otherwise the pressure cooker can struggle to go to pressure.)

06 Now create a tiered system inside the cooking pot. Use a trivet/rack with two tiers or you can place one trivet in lower position and one in top position. Place foil on the lower trivet and add the broccolini and cubed butternut squash. Now add the tall trivet and place another layer of foil on top, then add the salmon fillets, spreading them out so that do not overlap.

07 Secure the pressure cooker lid and set the valve to sealing. Pressure cook for 2 minutes, followed by a 3-minute delayed release.

08 Open the lid and transfer the salmon to a chopping board. Chop each salmon fillet into thirds. Season with salt and pepper, and squeeze lemon juice over the top. Add a sprinkling of dill.

09 Add the butternut squash to the bowl with the pearl barley, then add all the grain bowl ingredients. Mix well.

10 Place the pearl barley and squash in a serving bowl, then arrange the broccolini, hummus, halloumi, slaw and salmon on two plates to serve.

BEANS & LENTILS

NO SOAK DRIED BEANS

One of the biggest perks of owning a pressure cooker is how quickly you can turn dried beans into cooked and on your dinner plate. Smile and say goodbye to hours and hours of soaking your beans. Whether white, black or kidney beans, they can go straight in the pot and be pressure cooked.

The time can vary depending on the dried beans or peas. The longest is chickpeas and marrowfat peas at 40 minutes, while black beans and butter beans/lima beans are done in just 25 minutes.

Since we've learnt how easy it is to cook dried beans in the pressure cooker, it's become our go-to dinner. Let's get you started with some black beans, then you can fall in love with this method, too.

SERVES 6

PREP 2 MINS

SAUTE 0 MINS

PRESSURE COOK 25 MINS

RELEASE QPR

TOTAL COOK TIME 25 MINS

207 CALS

25-MINUTE BLACK BEANS

370g/13oz/2 cups dried black beans
600ml/21fl oz/2½ cups cold vegetable stock

01 Rinse the black beans in a colander under a cold tap.

02 Tip the beans into the cooking pot and pour in the vegetable stock. Season generously with salt and pepper.

03 Secure the pressure cooker lid and set the valve to sealing. Pressure cook for 25 minutes, followed by a quick pressure release.

04 After releasing the remaining pressure, remove the lid and stir the beans. Drain them and they are ready for serving.

BEANS & LENTILS COOKING TIMES

Now you have pressure-cooked black beans without soaking, why not experiment with other beans and lentils. Everything here uses QPR, just remember to adjust the ratios and cooking times.

Adzuki beans 200g/1 cup beans, 720ml/3 cups liquid, 20 minutes

Black-eyed beans 400g/2 cups beans, 600ml/2½ cups liquid, 30 minutes

Brown lentils 210g/1 cup lentils, 480ml/2 cups liquid, 10 minutes

Butter/lima beans 400g/2 cups beans, 600ml/2½ cups liquid, 25 minutes

Chickpeas 380g/2 cups chickpeas, 1.4litres/6 cups liquid, 40 minutes

Green lentils 200g/1 cup lentils, 480ml/2 cups liquid, 10 minutes

Green split peas 215g/1 cup peas, 480ml/2 cups liquid, 15 minutes

Kidney beans 370g/2 cups beans, 600ml/2½ cups liquid, 30 minutes

Marrow fat peas 210g/1 cup peas, 480ml/2 cups liquid, 40 minutes

Mixed lentils (good for soups or curry) 220g/1 cup mixed lentils, 480ml/2 cups liquid, 8 minutes

Mung beans 180g/1 cup beans, 720ml/3 cups liquid, 10 minutes

Pearl barley 200g/1 cup pearl barley, 480ml/2 cups liquid, 18 minutes

Pinto beans 190g/1 cup beans, 720ml/3 cups liquid, 20 minutes

White beans i.e. haricot 380g/2 cups beans, 600ml/2½ cups liquid, 35 minutes

Yellow split peas 200g/1 cup peas, 480ml/2 cups liquid, 15 minutes

SERVES
4

PREP
8 MINS

SAUTE
0 MINS

PRESSURE COOK
40 MINS

RELEASE
QPR

TOTAL COOK TIME
40 MINS

366 CALS

TAKE-TO-WORK MIXED BEAN SALAD

So, you've ticked off the bucket list cooking various beans in the pressure cooker without soaking them first. But what about making a meal with your new bean cooking skills? Load cooked beans into Tupperware with our Mediterranean salad ingredients and make a simple dressing and you have 4 portions ready for work. As the prep takes place in your Tupperware, you have less washing up!

200g/7oz/1 cup mixed dried beans (we use ¼ cup each of dried chickpeas, black-eyed beans, black beans and haricot beans)
480ml/17fl oz/2 cups cold vegetable stock
200g/7oz cherry tomatoes
½ large cucumber
1 medium yellow (bell) pepper/capsicum
1 small red onion
2 celery sticks
200g/7oz feta cheese

SALAD DRESSING
2 tbsp white wine vinegar
2 tbsp balsamic vinegar
1 tbsp extra virgin olive oil
1 tbsp fresh lime juice
2 tsp finely chopped fresh basil, plus extra leaves to serve

01 Rinse the beans and tip into the cooking pot, pour in the vegetable stock, stir and secure the pressure cooker lid. Set the valve to sealing and pressure cook for 40 minutes, followed by a quick pressure release.

02 Drain the cooked beans and transfer them to a large Tupperware container (ours is about 3 litres/3.17 quarts).

03 Cut the cherry tomatoes into quarters and add them to the beans. Slice the cucumber, pepper, onion and celery into bite-sized pieces, and add to the beans as you prep them. Crumble the feta and add to the beans, too. Mix well.

04 In a little Tupperware container or jar, mix the salad dressing ingredients. When you are ready to serve your salad, portion it up, add the dressing and sprinkle over a few extra basil leaves. The salad once it is dressed will last 1 day, but by keeping it separate the salad will last 4 days.

Mixed Beans Cooking Times You'll notice that we use mixed beans and individually they have different cooking times. How it works is we cook them all for however the longest bean cooking time is. We also adjusted the liquid ratio quantities to match the one that needs the most amount of liquid.

Build Your Own Bean Salad Mix and match your salad ingredients. Hate peppers? Swap for more cucumber. Why not include some grated carrot or some sliced radishes, too?

ROAST PEPPER & HARISSA HUMMUS

SERVES
6

PREP
5 MINS

SAUTE
8 MINS

PRESSURE COOK
40 MINS

RELEASE
QPR

TOTAL COOK TIME
48 MINS

147 CALS

Pressure-cooked dried chickpeas (no need to soak first), blended in a food processor with sautéed peppers and harissa – this is a great homemade version of the classic.

- 720ml/24⅓fl oz/3 cups cold vegetable stock
- 185g/6½oz/1 cup dried chickpeas
- 2 red (bell) peppers/capsicums
- 1½ tbsp extra virgin olive oil
- 1 tbsp harissa paste
- 2 tsp tomato purée/paste
- 1 tbsp garlic purée
- 4 tbsp fresh lemon juice
- 4 tsp smoked paprika, plus extra to serve

01 Pour the stock into the cooking pot, then add the dried chickpeas. Secure the pressure cooker lid and set the valve to sealing. Pressure cook for 40 minutes, followed by a quick pressure release.

02 Carefully open the lid, and use a mesh strainer to drain the chickpeas. Have a bowl underneath to catch the liquid, as you'll be using some of this later.

03 Press sauté on the cooking pot and let it warm up as you prep. Slice the peppers into little chunks about 1cm/½in square. Discard the seeds and add the chunks to the cooking pot along with half the olive oil.

04 Once the peppers are starting to crisp, cancel the sauté, add the harissa and tomato and garlic purées, and give it a good stir with a wooden spoon. Pour in 4 tablespoons of the reserved cooking liquid and stir again. It should have a consistency similar to chutney.

05 Place the roasted pepper mixture in a food processor with the chickpeas, reserving a handful to garnish. Add another 4 tablespoons of the reserved cooking liquid, the lemon juice, smoked paprika and a generous seasoning of salt and pepper. Blend until smooth, adding a little extra cooking liquid, if needed. Remember you can add more but you can't take it away, so adjust slowly to your desired creamy texture.

06 Sauté the reserved chickpeas in the remaining olive oil.

07 Serve the hummus topped with the sautéed chickpeas and a sprinkling of paprika, with some sliced red pepper, carrot and celery sticks alongside.

Dried Chickpeas vs Canned Chickpeas If you have never pressure cooked dried chickpeas before, then note they have a different texture to canned beans. They won't have been sitting in a can of liquid for months on a supermarket shelf waiting to be picked! This means they are a little drier and, when making hummus, you'll find yourself using slightly more liquid. You will also find yourself needing a good-quality food processor or blender to mix them. But they are so worth it – when you try the great flavour of homemade hummus you won't look back.

SERVES
6

PREP
6 MINS

SAUTE
5 MINS

PRESSURE COOK
5 MINS

RELEASE
QPR

TOTAL COOK TIME
10 MINS

480 CALS

CHILLI CON CARNE

On page 90 we showed you how easy it is to cook your own dried beans. But let's put it into practice by cooking some kidney beans first, then transforming it into a delicious big pot of chilli con carne. If you are vegetarian or vegan, follow our meatless recipe opposite.

1 medium brown onion
1 red (bell) pepper/capsicum
1 tbsp extra virgin olive oil
3 large tomatoes
1kg/2lb 4oz minced/ground beef
360ml/12fl oz/1½ cups cold beef stock
185g/6½oz/1 cup cooked kidney beans (see page 91)
500g/1lb 2oz/2 cups passata

CHILLI SPICE MIX
4 tsp ground cumin
4 tsp smoked paprika
2 tsp garlic powder
1 tbsp dried oregano
2 tsp cayenne pepper (adjust to taste)
1 tsp soft brown sugar

01 Make the spice mix by placing the herbs and spices in a small bowl and stirring to combine.

02 Peel and dice the onion. Deseed and dice the pepper. Press sauté, then add the chopped onion and pepper to the pot with the olive oil.

03 Meanwhile, chop the tomatoes, then add these, too. Continue to sauté until the tomatoes have softened, then add the mince, breaking it up as it cooks.

04 When the mince is almost brown, cancel the sauté, pour in the beef stock, and add a quarter of the spice mix and the kidney beans. Stir well.

05 Secure the pressure cooker lid and set the valve to sealing. Pressure cook for 5 minutes, followed by a quick pressure release.

06 When the pressure cooker beeps, release the remaining pressure and add the remaining spice mix. Stir in the passata (it will warm through in the heat of the pot) and season with salt and pepper to serve.

Batch the Chilli Why not make chilli freezer cubes? You could then have chilli in the freezer with the jacket potatoes for another day.

SERVES
6

PREP
10 MINS

SAUTE
8 MINS

PRESSURE COOK
0 MINS

RELEASE
QPR

TOTAL COOK TIME
8 MINS

125 CALS

- 1 medium brown onion
- 1 medium aubergine/eggplant
- 1 medium courgette/zucchini
- 1 red (bell) pepper/capsicum
- 1 tbsp extra virgin olive oil
- 1 garlic bulb
- 4 large tomatoes
- 360ml/12fl oz/1½ cups cold vegetable stock
- 1 tbsp tomato purée/paste
- 90g/3¼oz/½ cup cooked black eyed beans (see page 91)
- 90g/3¼oz/½ cup cooked kidney beans (see page 91)
- 500g/1lb 2oz/2 cups passata
- Handful of roughly chopped kale
- 1 tbsp roughly chopped fresh basil

MAKE-AHEAD VEGAN BEAN RAGU

I have been a vegetarian in a meat household and we have many readers in a similar boat. It's hard when you have to make 2 different types of meal, based on different diet lifestyles. That's why we've made the chilli con carne opposite and this vegan bean ragu. If the dinner on offer is not meat-free, you can fall back on your big batch of this yummy ragu. Freeze it like we do our mince cubes on page 183. It's loaded with beans and veg, is filling, healthy and satisfying all at the same time.

01 Peel and dice the onion, chop the aubergine into chunks, slice the courgette into medium chunks, and deseed and dice the pepper.

02 Press sauté, then add the chopped veg and a drizzle of olive oil.

03 Meanwhile, chop the top and bottom from the garlic bulb (this makes it easier to peel). Peel the garlic cloves then slice them thinly. Chop each tomato into 8 pieces. Add the sliced garlic and chopped tomato to the cooking pot and continue to sauté, sweating out the veg. When the tomatoes are soft, press cancel. Deglaze the cooking pot with the vegetable stock, stir and scrape any bits stuck to the bottom and sides.

04 Stir in the tomato purée and the cooked beans. Secure the pressure cooker lid and set the valve to sealing. Pressure cook for 0 minutes, followed by a quick pressure release.

05 When the pressure cooker beeps, release the remaining pressure and stir in the passata (it will warm through in the heat of the pot). Add a generous seasoning of salt and pepper, and stir in the basil before serving.

SERVES
4

PREP
6 MINS

SAUTE
0 MINS

PRESSURE COOK
15 MINS

RELEASE
CR

TOTAL COOK TIME
15 MINS

443 CALS

RED THAI CURRY LENTILS

This is my all-time favourite lentil recipe for the pressure cooker. I often make a batch of it, then warm it up for my lunch. Made with green lentils and your favourite red Thai curry flavours, it's fast, easy and freezes well, too.

1 medium brown onion, diced
300g/10½oz/1½ cups dried green lentils
480ml/17fl oz/2 cups cold vegetable stock
2 heaped tbsp red Thai curry paste
1 heaped tbsp garlic purée
1 heaped tbsp ginger purée
1 tbsp garam masala
1 tsp ground coriander
½ tsp turmeric
2 tbsp mango chutney
500g/1lb 2oz/2 cups passata
240ml/8½fl oz/1 cup coconut milk
Roughly chopped fresh coriander/cilantro

01 Add the onion, lentils, vegetable stock, curry paste, garlic and ginger purées, dried spices and half the mango chutney to the cooking pot and give it all a really good stir. Pour in the passata without stirring.

02 Secure the pressure cooker lid and set the valve to sealing. Pressure cook for 15 minutes, followed by a 10-minute controlled/pulse pressure release.

03 Add the remaining mango chutney and the coconut milk and season generously with salt and pepper. Give it a good stir. You should have creamy lentils with a slight bite to them. Serve sprinkled with fresh coriander.

A Thick Red Thai Curry Sauce Thanks to the green lentils, you can blend the leftovers until smooth and you'll have a lovely, thick curry sauce for your next red Thai curry feast.

Why Green Lentils? I often get asked why green lentils are so popular in the pressure cooker. It is because they pressure cook well and don't go to mush. They also have a lovely bite to them, so add a nice texture to your meal.

KITTY'S RAPID MUSHY PEAS

SERVES 4

PREP 3 MINS

SAUTE 0 MINS

PRESSURE COOK 10 MINS

RELEASE DR

TOTAL COOK TIME 10 MINS

256 CALS

225g/8oz/1 cup green split peas
480ml/17fl oz/2 cups vegetable stock
2 tbsp salted butter
1 tbsp fresh lemon juice

Mushy peas made in a pressure cooker have a place close to my heart. This is what my grandma would make in her old stovetop pressure cooker and, if it went wrong, we'd end up with a green ceiling! Traditional mushy peas made with marrowfat peas take 40 minutes; this version using green split peas takes just 10 minutes.

01 Tip the split peas and stock into the cooking pot. Chop the butter into small chunks and place over the peas (the butter will melt into the peas as they cook).

02 Secure the pressure cooker lid and set the valve to sealing. Pressure cook for 10 minutes, followed by a 5-minute delayed pressure release.

03 When the pressure cooker beeps, release the remaining pressure and add the lemon juice and a generous seasoning of salt and pepper. Stir and serve.

Mushy Peas Cubes Mushy peas are one of those 'love or hate' foods. If you love them but your family doesn't, portion up a batch and freeze it in cubes. You can just defrost a portion whenever you fancy mushy peas.

MUSHY PEAS CURRY FOR TWO

SERVES 2

PREP 8 MINS

SAUTE 5 MINS

PRESSURE COOK 2 MINS

RELEASE QPR

TOTAL COOK TIME 7 MINS

510 CALS

225g/8oz tenderstem broccoli
225g/8oz butternut squash, cut into 2cm/¾in cubes (prepared weight)
⅓ × portion Kitty's rapid mushy peas (see above)
500g/1lb 2oz/2 cups passata
½ × 400g/14oz can coconut milk
4 tsp each ginger purée, garlic purée and tikka masala paste
1 heaped tsp curry powder
1 tsp garam masala

This is a twist on the classic 90s diet club trend using the mushy peas recipe above, passata, coconut milk and your favourite curry flavourings.

01 Pour 240ml/8½fl oz/1 cup water into the cooking pot. Add the steamer basket, then add the broccoli and butternut squash.

02 Secure the pressure cooker lid and set the valve to sealing. Pressure cook for 2 minutes, followed by a quick pressure release.

03 Carefully open the lid, then lift out the steamer basket and put the veg to one side. Discard the liquid from the cooking pot.

04 Press sauté, then add the cooled mushy peas, passata and coconut milk to the cooking pot. Use a wooden spoon to stir and break up the mushy peas until it is a creamy, lump-free sauce. Press cancel, add the remaining ingredients and stir until they are all well combined. Finally, return the cooked veg to the pot, season with salt and pepper, give it one last stir and serve.

Mix & Match What we love most about this curry is how adaptable it is. Swap a mild curry powder for a Caribbean spice mix or a hot Madras. You could also swap the veg for chicken (use the cooking time from page 50).

PASTA & GRAINS

HOW TO PRESSURE COOK ANY PASTA

Pasta and grains provide pressure cooker owners with magical moments. When that pressure cooker beeps and you have perfect grains, it always brings a smile to your face. Pasta, rice, quinoa and pearl barley are just a few of the grains that cook well in the pressure cooker. In this chapter we begin by sharing some of our favourite pasta recipes. We start with a seafood linguine, then share the easiest-ever mac and cheese, and finally introduce you to a pressure cooker favourite – lasagne pie.

MANY PASTAS ONE COOKING TIME!

One thing that surprises people is that many types of dried pasta have the same cooking time. This means it is super easy to convert pasta recipes from one kind of pasta to another. This linguine method will also work with spaghetti, macaroni, spirali, farfalle, rigatoni or tagliatelle.

CHEESY PRAWN LINGUINE

SERVES
4

PREP
5 MINS

SAUTE
6 MINS

PRESSURE COOK
0 MINS

RELEASE
CR

TOTAL COOK TIME
6 MINS

425 CALS

- 225g/8oz dried linguine
- 960ml/32½fl oz/4 cups cold fish stock
- 1 tsp salt
- 250g/9oz raw, peeled super king prawns/shrimp
- 1 × 150g/5½oz pack garlic and herb cream cheese (we use Boursin)
- 1 heaped tbsp crème fraîche
- 80ml/2½fl oz/⅓ cup dry white wine
- 1 tbsp garlic purée
- 2 tbsp roughly chopped fresh parsley
- Lemon, to serve

01 Break the linguine in half and tip the pasta into the cooking pot. Pour in the fish stock and add the salt. Stir well. The stock will cover the pasta.

02 Secure the pressure cooker lid and set the valve to sealing. Pressure cook for 0 minutes, followed by a 10-minute controlled/pulse pressure release.

03 Open the lid, remove the pasta and set aside. Discard the cooking liquid, reserving 2 tablespoons to use later. (If you don't want to throw all the stock away, you could also keep it to use another day.) Press sauté and add the prawns, garlic and herb cheese, crème fraîche and white wine to the pot. Stir until the prawns are a beautiful shade of pink.

04 Stir the garlic purée, the reserved pasta water and the parsley into the sauce, then return the linguine to the pot. Cancel sauté. Stir the pasta into your cream sauce, season with black pepper, and serve with a squeeze or two of lemon.

TRIPLE CHEESE MAC & CHEESE

SERVES 4

PREP 8 MINS

SAUTE 0 MINS

PRESSURE COOK 0 MINS

RELEASE CR

TOTAL COOK TIME 0 MINS

787 CALS

This is the mac and cheese of your dreams. Three different cheeses and no separate cheese sauce to make because everything happens in one cooking pot. Just the right amount of liquid is added, so you don't need to drain the pasta after cooking.

- 450g/1lb/4 cups dried macaroni
- 960ml/32½fl oz/4 cups cold vegetable stock
- 1 tsp salt
- 55g/2oz/¼ cup salted butter
- 1 tsp garlic mayonnaise
- 115g/4oz/1 cup grated mature/sharp Cheddar
- 85g/3oz/¾ cup grated red Leicester/Monterey Jack cheese
- 55g/2oz/generous ½ cup grated Parmesan
- 4 tbsp semi-skimmed/2% fat milk

01 Tip the macaroni into the cooking pot and pour in the vegetable stock. Add the salt and stir. The stock will cover the pasta.

02 Secure the pressure cooker lid and set the valve to sealing. Pressure cook for 0 minutes, followed by a 10-minute controlled/pulse pressure release.

03 Open the lid and season generously with pepper. Add the butter, garlic mayo and all the cheeses, and give it a good stir. The residual heat in the cooking pot will be enough – you don't have to put it on sauté.

04 Gradually add the milk, stirring all the time. It's now ready to serve!

Al Dente Pasta Because we will be stirring in extra ingredients after cooking the pasta, we are only just cooking the macaroni. This is done with a 0-minute cooking time, then letting it sit so it can continue cooking slowly.

Pulled Pork Mac & Cheese This is delicious and brings together two of the best comfort foods of all time. Place 480g/1lb 1oz/3 cups leftover macaroni cheese in the cooking pot. Add 240ml/8½fl oz/1 cup milk and press sauté. As it warms up, the milk will help make the macaroni creamy again. In the meantime, stir in 150g/5oz/1½ cups grated Cheddar and 360g/12½oz/2 cups pulled pork. Sprinkle in salt, pepper, a little smoked paprika and some dried oregano. Serve once the pulled pork has warmed through.

SERVES
6

PREP
12 MINS

SAUTE
10 MINS

PRESSURE COOK
15 MINS

RELEASE
QPR

TOTAL COOK TIME
25 MINS

696 CALS

LASAGNE PIE

Go to lasagne heaven with this lasagne that is layered and cooked in a springform tin. It is truly delicious and so easy to make. We make the Bolognese first using the sauté function, then load it with our cheese sauce from page 136.

1 medium brown onion
1 tbsp extra virgin olive oil
750g/1lb 10oz minced/ground beef (we use 5% fat)
2 tsp tomato purée/paste
Handful of fresh basil leaves, finely chopped
4 thyme sprigs, leaves picked
500g/1lb 2oz/2 cups tomato & red pepper sauce (see page 136), or passata
Olive oil spray, for greasing
4–6 fresh lasagne sheets
240ml/8½fl oz/1 cup homemade cheese sauce (see page 136)
28g/1oz/⅓ cup grated Parmesan

01 Peel and dice the onion, and add it to the cooking pot with the olive oil. Press sauté and cook until your onion is starting to soften. Add the mince, breaking it down with a wooden spoon as you sauté.

02 When the mince has browned, add the tomato purée, basil, thyme and the tomato and red pepper sauce, and season well with salt and pepper. When the mince is cooked, press cancel and take the cooking pot out of the cooker.

03 Spray the bottom and sides of an 18cm/7in springform tin/pan with olive oil. Cut the lasagne sheets to the size of your tin. Fresh lasagne is brilliant as it's so easy to cut to size and it cooks more quickly.

04 Assemble the lasagne. Start at the very bottom with a layer of lasagne sheets, this stops the Bolognese spilling. Now add a layer of Bolognese, then your second lasagne sheet layer, then more Bolognese. Add a third lasagne sheet layer, then more Bolognese, and finally a fourth lasagne sheet layer. Top with the cheese sauce and a sprinkling of Parmesan. Place a layer of foil over the tin. (If you have any leftover Bolognese you can save this for another day.)

05 Pour 240ml/8½fl oz/1 cup cold water into the dirty cooking pot. Scrape the bottom and sides with a wooden spoon. (As you pressure cook, the cooking pot will get its first clean, making it easier for you to clean later.) Add a trivet/rack to the pot and place the tin with your lasagne on top. Secure the pressure cooker lid and set the valve to sealing. Pressure cook for 15 minutes, followed by a quick pressure release.

06 Open the lid and remove the foil from the tin. Let the lasagne cool in the tin for 10 minutes before serving with basil leaves, some lettuce and don't forget a glass of red wine!

Enchiladas Lasagne Pie Make the pie as above, except you should add 1 diced red (bell) pepper/capsicum and 1 deseeded, finely diced green jalapeño when you sauté the onion. Swap the tomato and red pepper sauce for an equal quantity of mild salsa. Make the taco seasoning as page 74 and add three-quarters to the mince, then a quarter to the cheese sauce. Swap the layers of lasagne for mini tortillas, cut to the size of your springform tin/pan. On the final stir of the mince, also add in 1 cup of frozen sweetcorn and 1 cup of cooked black beans.

SERVES
4

PREP
3 MINS

SAUTE
0 MINS

PRESSURE COOK
18 MINS

RELEASE
DR

TOTAL COOK TIME
18 MINS

223 CALS

BROWN RICE 101

After pasta, it's time to learn rice. Rice cooks in a similar way to pasta in the pressure cooker. You add rice, water or stock and pressure cook. That perfect ratio of rice to liquid leads to perfect fluffy rice. But our all-time favourite rice to pressure cook is brown rice. It may take longer to cook long-grain brown rice than regular white rice, but it never fails, looks good and is very flavourful. If I could just cook one rice forever in the pressure cooker it would be this.

- 200g/7oz/1 cup long-grain brown rice, rinsed
- 360ml/12fl oz/1½ cups cold vegetable stock
- 1 tbsp salted butter, chopped into chunks
- 1 tsp garlic powder
- 2 tbsp roughly chopped fresh coriander/cilantro

01 Tip the brown rice into the cooking pot and pour in the vegetable stock.

02 Secure the pressure cooker lid and set the valve to sealing. Pressure cook for 18 minutes, followed by a 5-minute delayed pressure release.

03 Open the lid and season generously with salt and pepper. Stir in the butter, garlic and coriander, and fluff it up with a silicone spatula before serving.

MORE RICE COOKING TIMES

Basmati white rice 1 cup rice, 1½ cups liquid, 3 mins, 10dr
Basmati brown rice 1 cup rice, 1½ cups liquid, 10 mins, 10dr
Jasmine rice 1½ cups rice, 2 cups liquid, 3 mins, 10dr
Long-grain white rice 1 cup rice, 1½ cups liquid, 3 mins, 10dr
Sushi 1 cup rice, 1 cup liquid, 6 mins, 10dr

These quantities would serve 4 when paired with your favourite protein.

SERVES
4

PREP
2 MINS

SAUTE
0 MINS

PRESSURE COOK
1 MIN

RELEASE
DR

TOTAL COOK TIME
1 MIN

161 CALS

NO FAIL QUINOA

Quinoa was the first grain I ever cooked under pressure. I was amazed by how ridiculously easy it was. It's 10 minutes faster to cook than brown rice, so why not have it as your 'I haven't got time to cook' recipe?

- 190g/6¾oz/1 cup quinoa
- 360ml/12fl oz/1¼ cups cold vegetable stock

01 Tip the quinoa into the cooking pot and pour in the vegetable stock. Season with salt and pepper.

02 Secure the pressure cooker lid and set the valve to sealing. Pressure cook for 1 minute, followed a 12-minute delayed release.

03 Open the lid and stir the quinoa with a silicone spatula before serving.

SERVES
4

PREP
8 MINS

SAUTE
0 MINS

PRESSURE COOK
5 MINS

RELEASE
DR

TOTAL COOK TIME
5 MINS

492 CALS

BUILD A BURRITO BAR

Grab your favourite serving platter and let's build a burrito bar. All your favourite burrito fillings are made into a mini buffet for four. Perfect for your next movie night. You'll love our shortcuts for making this faster.

- 4 corn on the cobettes
- 2 medium skinless and boneless chicken breasts
- ½ quantity cooked long-grain brown rice (see page 110)
- ½ quantity cooked black beans (see page 90)
- 2 limes, halved
- 1 medium avocado, sliced
- Roughly chopped fresh coriander/cilantro
- 1 red chilli, sliced (optional)
- Selection of Tex Mex dips (we use guacamole, salsa and sour cream)

CHIPOTLE SAUCE

- 2 tsp chipotle paste
- ½ tsp each onion powder and garlic powder
- 1 tsp smoked paprika
- 1 tsp ground cumin
- 1 tbsp fresh lime juice
- 1 heaped tbsp sour cream

01 Pour 240ml/8½fl oz/1 cup cold water into the cooking pot and add the corn on the cobettes. Place the trivet/rack in the pot.

02 Add all the chipotle sauce ingredients to a bowl and mix well. Add the chicken breasts and mix again so the chicken is well coated. Add a layer of foil to the trivet, then place the chicken with its marinade on too.

03 Secure the pressure cooker lid and set the valve to sealing. Pressure cook for 5 minutes, followed by a 5-minute delayed pressure release.

04 Meanwhile, assemble your burrito platter. Place the brown rice, black beans and lime on the platter. We like to put the dips into little serving dishes.

05 When the chicken is done, open the lid, remove the chicken and cut into thick slices. Remove the corn from the pot and slice the kernels from the cobs, by standing them on their ends, then slicing down the sides.

06 Add the corn to the beans and place the slices of chicken on the platter. Top with the avocado, then drizzle with the leftover cooked marinade. Squeeze some lime juice over the chicken and sprinkle with the coriander and chilli, if using. Serve with the dips and some tortilla chips.

SOFIA & JORGE'S HOMEMADE SUSHI

SERVES
4

PREP
10 MINS

SAUTE
0 MINS

PRESSURE COOK
6 MINS

RELEASE
DR

TOTAL COOK TIME
6 MINS

484 CALS

When they were 9 and 7, Sofia and Jorge learnt how to make sushi at baking class. It was great fun and started an obsession. This is their recipe for sushi and dragon rolls. But first let them show you how to cook sushi rice in the pressure cooker.

450g/1lb/2 cups sushi rice, rinsed
480ml/17fl oz/2 cups cold vegetable stock
5 sheets nori (seaweed)
Soy sauce, for dipping

FILLINGS

3 tbsp cold shredded chicken (we use chicken curry on page 56)
½ avocado
¼ medium cucumber
1 slice smoked salmon
2 tbsp cream cheese

VINEGAR MIX

2 tbsp white wine vinegar
1 tsp granulated sugar
½ tsp salt

01 Tip the sushi rice into the cooking pot and pour in the vegetable stock.

02 Secure the pressure cooker lid and set the valve to sealing. Pressure cook for 6 minutes, followed by a 10-minute delayed release.

03 Open the lid and stir the rice with a silicone spatula. Before the rice has a chance to cool, combine the vinegar mix ingredients in a small bowl, then stir it into the rice. Remove the cooking pot and set aside so the sushi rice can cool.

04 In the meantime, plan your fillings. We use leftover shredded chicken in sauce from page 56. By using sauce, it stops the sushi from being too dry. We also chopped avocado and cucumber into very small chunks. Finally, we rolled some with smoked salmon and cream cheese. You can mix and match with whatever you have, such as tuna mayonnaise, crabsticks etc.

05 When the rice is cool, cover a bamboo rolling mat with cling film/plastic wrap. Place a sheet of nori on top. Cover the nori with a layer of rice, but leave a 1.5cm/⅝in border around the edges. Be firm so that it stays in place. You're aiming for a thin layer of rice. Too thick and you will struggle to roll it.

06 Depending on your choice of filling, either create a line of avocado chunks, then a line of cumber; or spoon a thin layer of the chicken curry leftovers on to the rice – being careful not to make it too thick; or add a single layer of salmon, then spread over the cream cheese. Whichever you choose, make sure to cover the bottom third of the rice. Once your choice of filling has been added, roll up the sushi, making sure the filling is in the centre and the bamboo mat is rolling away from you as you roll.

07 Slice the roll into bite-sized pieces using a sharp knife with serrated edges. Serve with pickled ginger and soy sauce, for dipping.

Sushi & Vinegar Sushi translates as rice with vinegar. To get the texture right, make sure it's still warm when you add your vinegar mix.

Sushi Filling You can add any filling you like. As shown in the photo opposite, we made chicken curry dragon rolls, smoked salmon and cream cheese, and cucumber sushi, but you could use leftovers from many recipes in this book.

SERVES
4

PREP
8 MINS

SAUTE
10 MINS

PRESSURE COOK
3 MINS

RELEASE
DR

TOTAL COOK TIME
13 MINS

470 CALS

TEPPANYAKI-INSPIRED EGG-FRIED RICE

Whilst on holiday in Mexico, the hotel we were staying in had various themed restaurants, and one of them was a teppanyaki place. It was the kids' first experience of it, and their faces lit up when the show cooking started. Sushi was made in front of us and the entertainment chef created flames on his grill before creating yummy rice. Why not serve this with the sushi from page 114.

- 200g/7oz/1 cup jasmine rice, rinsed
- 1 medium brown onion
- 1 tbsp extra virgin olive oil
- 375g/13oz protein of choice (we use a mix of raw super king prawns/shrimp, strips of steak and chicken)
- 2 tbsp salted butter
- 6 tbsp soy sauce
- 2 x 135g/4¾oz steam bags of vegetables (ours had frozen peas, sweetcorn, carrot and pepper)
- 2 large eggs

01 Pour 240ml/8½fl oz/1 cup cold water into the cooking pot and add the rice. Secure the pressure cooker lid and set the valve to sealing. Pressure cook for 3 minutes, followed by a 10-minute delayed pressure release. Remove the rice and set aside. (There's no need to clean the cooking pot as the odd bit is fine.)

02 Press sauté. Whilst the cooking pot is warming up, peel and dice the onion, then add it to the cooking pot with the olive oil. Scrape any bits of stuck on rice as you sauté.

03 Add your protein – whether that is prawns, beef or chicken, or a mixture of all three. (At a teppanyaki restaurant, you would be asked if you want a mix.)

04 Add the salted butter, 4 tablespoons of the soy sauce and all the veg to the pot. Give it a good stir until the chicken is cooked, the prawns are pink and the beef strips are cooked to your liking.

05 Push everything to one side of your cooking pot, then crack the eggs into the clear space you've made. Let them sit for a minute, then stir to create scrambled eggs. Once fully scrambled, press cancel, then stir to bring together all the ingredients in the cooking pot. Add of the remaining soy sauce and the rice, then stir a final time and serve.

Mix & Match Protein In a classic teppanyaki restaurant you would be offered prawns/shrimp, chicken and beef. At home, why not use some pork strips, halloumi for a vegetarian option or tofu for a vegan option?

ASPARAGUS & PARMESAN RISOTTO

SERVES
4

PREP
5 MINS

SAUTE
5 MINS

PRESSURE COOK
6 MINS

RELEASE
DR

TOTAL COOK TIME
11 MINS

420 CALS

- 250g/9oz asparagus spears
- 2 medium lemons
- 4 spring/green onions
- 2 tbsp salted butter, straight from the fridge
- 4 garlic cloves
- 120ml/4fl oz/½ cup dry white wine
- 960ml/34fl oz/4 cups cold vegetable stock
- 220g/8oz/1½ cups arborio rice, rinsed
- 100g/3½oz/1 cup grated Parmesan, plus extra to serve
- 1 tbsp crème fraîche
- 2 tsp dried oregano
- 2 tsp roughly chopped fresh parsley

Creamy deliciousness in a bowl. Made with asparagus, lemons and Parmesan cheese, you'll just have to have a second bowl of this wonderful comfort food.

01 Remove the woody ends from the asparagus, then slice the spears into thirds. Zest 1 lemon and set aside. Juice both lemons and set aside.

02 Slice the spring onions into medium chunks, add them to the cooking pot with the butter and press sauté. When the butter is almost melted, peel and thinly slice the garlic and add that, too. When the garlic is just softening, add the asparagus, stir, then press cancel.

03 Deglaze the cooking pot with the white wine, then pour in the stock. Scrape any bits stuck to the bottom and sides, then add the rice. Add three-quarters of the lemon juice to the pot and stir.

04 Secure the pressure cooker lid and set the valve to sealing. Pressure cook for 6 minutes, followed by a 10-minute delayed release.

05 Open the lid, stir in the remaining lemon juice, the grated Parmesan, crème fraîche and herbs. Season generously with salt and pepper, and serve with the lemon zest and some extra Parmesan sprinkled over the top.

SERVES
4

PREP
10 MINS

SAUTE
0 MINS

PRESSURE COOK
1 MIN

RELEASE
DR

TOTAL COOK TIME
1 MIN

618 CALS

190g/6¾oz/1 cup quinoa
360ml/12fl oz/1¼ cups cold vegetable stock

FOR THE SALAD
½ medium red onion
225g/8oz cherry tomatoes
½ large cucumber
1 yellow (bell) pepper/capsicum
1 large avocado
175g/6oz/1 cup cooked chickpeas
115g/4oz pitted black olives, sliced
50g/2oz/½ cup grated Parmesan

FOR THE SALAD DRESSING
4 tbsp extra virgin olive oil
¼ tsp white wine vinegar
2½ tsp balsamic vinegar
1 tsp Dijon mustard
1 tsp dried oregano
½ tsp garlic powder
2 tbsp runny honey

THE BIG CHOP QUINOA SALAD

The perfect summer salad. Ingredients are chopped to a similar size, hence the name, all whilst the quinoa is cooking in the pressure cooker. Get out your favourite salad bowl and let's make a quinoa salad!

01 Tip the quinoa into the cooking pot and pour in the vegetable stock. Season with salt and pepper.

02 Secure the pressure cooker lid and set the valve to sealing. Pressure cook for 1 minute, followed by a 12-minute delayed pressure release.

03 Meanwhile, let's make the salad. Peel and chop the red onion, halve the cherry tomatoes, chop the cucumber, deseed and chop the pepper, and remove the stone and peel and chop the avocado. Chop all the ingredients to a similar 2cm/¾in size.

04 In a jug, combine all the dressing ingredients and mix with a fork.

05 When the quinoa is ready, open the lid and stir with a silicone spatula.

06 Spread the quinoa across the bottom of a large salad bowl. Pile the onion, tomatoes, cucumber, avocado and pepper on top, keeping each ingredient in its own little section. Add more little piles with the chickpeas, black olives and grated cheese.

07 Finish by drizzling your dressing over the salad. If you're not serving the salad straight away, store the dressing in a container and add it just before serving (this will make the salad last longer).

SOUPS & SAUCES

YOUR FIRST PRESSURE COOKER SOUP

Pressure cookers are a soup lover's soul mate. With a large cooking pot and a quick cooking time for lots of soup staple ingredients, it is effortless to make a pot of soup. You can use the pressure cooker for chunky soups, smooth soups, chowder, or even soup loaded with dried beans, lentils or meat or fish.

For your first attempt, we recommend trying a creamy vegetable soup. They are the easiest to prep, you can learn about the ratio of liquid to vegetables and, most importantly, cooking times.

Let's start with a carrot and ginger soup. It's a brilliant beginner soup and I love this so much I batch cook extra for the freezer for another day.

CARROT & GINGER SOUP

SERVES
6

PREP
10 MINS

SAUTE
0 MINS

PRESSURE COOK
12 MINS

RELEASE
QPR

TOTAL COOK TIME
12 MINS

230 CALS

- 1.35kg/3lb carrots
- 1 medium red onion
- 1 tbsp garlic purée
- 2 tbsp ginger purée
- 2 tbsp ground coriander
- 2 tbsp dried coriander/cilantro leaf
- 720ml/24⅓fl oz/3 cups cold vegetable stock
- 1 × 400g/14oz can full-fat coconut milk

01 Peel and dice the carrots and red onion into medium chunks, then add them to the cooking pot.

02 Add the garlic, ginger and corianders to the pot, and mix with your hands so there is a good coating of the flavours on the vegetables.

03 Pour in the vegetable stock, secure the pressure cooker lid and set the valve to sealing. Pressure cook for 12 minutes, followed by a quick pressure release.

04 After releasing the pressure, pour in the coconut milk, season generously with salt and pepper, and blend with a stick blender until smooth.

Freezer Soup Cubes Allow to cool completely then pour into individual containers (we use silicone soup cubes – see page 20). Secure the lid and freeze overnight. The next day, transfer the frozen soup portions/cubes to freezer bags. We made 4 × 480ml/17fl oz/2 cup cubes with this soup.

TOP TIPS

Cooking Time Is Key If you're aiming for a smooth, creamy soup, the cooking time is going to be longer. However, if you want just-cooked vegetables, then a shorter cooking time is required. Think about what kind of soup you'd like before setting the cooking time.

Pairing Ingredients You need to find a balance of ingredients that will be ready at the same time (see the orzo soup on page 128 as an example). However, if you want a smooth soup, then it's fine to pair root vegetables with lentils or split peas, as it won't matter that you are cooking them for a bit longer than usual.

Avoid Dishwasher Water This is chef speak for watered-down, flavourless soup. It's all about not adding too much liquid when you make the soup. It's easily done when you are experimenting with ratios. We recommend you start by following our carrot soup recipe, then try swapping the carrots for another root veg, keeping the same liquid ratio and you will see how easy it is to switch it up.

Thick vs Thin Ingredients Aim for balance. Don't use too many watery vegetables, and make sure there's enough liquid for root veg. If making a courgette soup, for example, add a potato to help thicken it.

A Partial Blend If you want a chunky soup but you also want it creamy, then partially blend the soup. Blending a quarter of the soup ingredients can make a huge difference to the creaminess, so there's no need to add actual cream as well.

Freezer Soup Bags Freeze the soup in 15 × 20cm/6 × 8in freezer bags. Lay them flat in the freezer with all the air removed. If freezing multiple bags, separate them with kitchen/paper towel; this will stop them sticking together. Remove the soup from the freezer bag with scissors. Pour 240ml/8½fl oz/1 cup cold vegetable stock into the cooking pot, then place the frozen block of soup inside at an angle. As it defrosts, it will melt into the stock. Secure the lid and set the valve to sealing. Pressure cook for 8 minutes, followed by a quick pressure release. Stir and serve.

GOLDEN CAULIFLOWER SOUP

SERVES
4

PREP
5 MINS

SAUTE
3 MINS

PRESSURE COOK
10 MINS

RELEASE
QPR

TOTAL COOK TIME
13 MINS

320 CALS

- 1 medium brown onion
- 2.5cm/1in piece of fresh root ginger
- 4 garlic cloves
- 1 tbsp extra virgin olive oil
- 1 tsp turmeric
- 720ml/24⅓fl oz/3 cups cold vegetable stock
- 1.2kg/3lb frozen cauliflower florets
- 1 × 400g/14oz can full-fat coconut milk
- 1 tbsp roughly chopped fresh coriander/cilantro
- 2 tsp ground cumin
- 2 tsp garam masala, plus extra to garnish

This is your everything soup. It's a creamy curry soup, it's a low-prep soup (thanks to using frozen cauliflower), your kids will actually eat it, and it combines Indian and Thai flavours for when you can't decide between the two. But what I love most is its elegant golden colour, thanks to the turmeric.

01 Peel and dice the onion into medium chunks. Peel and thinly slice the ginger and garlic. Press sauté on the pressure cooker, to give the cooking pot a chance to warm up.

02 Add the onion to the cooking pot, along with the olive oil. Sauté until the onion has softened.

03 Press cancel, then stir in the garlic, ginger and turmeric, and pour in the vegetable stock. Stir and use your wooden spoon to deglaze the cooking pot.

04 Tip the cauliflower into the pot, on top of the onion mixture, and don't stir. Secure the pressure cooker lid and set the valve to sealing. Pressure cook for 10 minutes followed by a quick pressure release.

05 After releasing the pressure, pour in the coconut milk, reserving a few teaspoons, and stir in the coriander, cumin and garam masala. Season generously with salt and pepper, then use a stick blender to blend the soup. (You can half blend it, if you prefer a chunky soup.) Give it a final stir, then serve with a drizzle of the reserved coconut milk and a sprinkling of garam masala.

ORZO VEGETABLE SOUP

SERVES
6

PREP
8 MINS

SAUTE
0 MINS

PRESSURE COOK
3 MINS

RELEASE
DR

TOTAL COOK TIME
3 MINS

145 CALS

1 medium brown onion
4 medium carrots
1 medium sweet potato
4 celery sticks
1 medium courgette/zucchini
1 red (bell) pepper/capsicum
1.4l/48fl oz/6 cups cold vegetable stock
100g/3½oz/½ cup dried orzo pasta

AFTER PRESSURE COOKING

1 tbsp dried coriander/cilantro leaf
½ tsp turmeric
½ tsp ground ginger
1 tsp fennel seeds

In between the golden cauliflower soup and the chicken gnocchi soup sits this delicious orzo and vegetable soup. It's vegan and is perfect for when you're bored of the same old creamy soups and are looking for a broth-like texture. It's loaded with veg and the orzo pasta makes it nice and filling.

01 Prep all the vegetables. Peel and dice the onion, carrots and sweet potato into medium chunks. Clean and slice the celery. Dice the courgette, and deseed and chop the pepper into chunks.

02 Tip all the prepared veg into the cooking pot. Pour in the vegetable stock, add the orzo and stir. Secure the pressure cooker lid and set the valve to sealing. Pressure cook for 3 minutes, followed by a 20-minute delayed pressure release.

03 After releasing pressure, stir in the seasonings, including a generous amount of salt and pepper.

04 Serve in bowls with crusty bread.

A Note On Fennel Love it or loathe it, fennel is not everyone's cup of tea. If you are not a fan, you can swap it for dried cumin or increase the dried coriander/cilantro.

CREAMY CHICKEN GNOCCHI SOUP WITH CIABATTA CROUTONS

SERVES
6

PREP
10 MINS

SAUTE
5 MINS

PRESSURE COOK
5 MINS

RELEASE
CR

TOTAL COOK TIME
10 MINS

647 CALS

- 1 medium brown onion
- 5 medium carrots
- 3 celery sticks
- 1 tbsp extra virgin olive oil
- 480ml/17fl oz/2 cups dry white wine
- 720ml/24⅓fl oz/3 cups chicken stock
- 650g/1½lb skinless and boneless chicken breasts, diced
- 500g/1lb 2oz gnocchi
- 1 × 150g/5½oz pack garlic and herb cream cheese (we use Boursin)
- 55g/2oz/½ cup grated mature/sharp Cheddar
- 1 tsp garlic powder
- 2 tbsp dried thyme
- 4 tbsp roughly chopped fresh basil, plus a few extra leaves to garnish

CIABATTA CROUTONS

- 2 tsp garlic purée
- 3 tbsp extra virgin olive oil
- 2 tsp dried basil
- 1 ciabatta roll, chopped into chunks

This soup tastes so creamy and naughty that your kids will actually eat celery and onion without complaining!

01 To make the croutons, mix the garlic, olive oil and basil in a mixing bowl. Add the ciabatta chunks and toss to coat.

02 Place the cooking pot on sauté and, when it warms up, add the coated croutons and sauté for about 5 minutes until golden and crispy. Remove the croutons from the cooking pot and set aside.

03 Peel and dice the onion and carrots, then clean and slice the celery. Transfer the prepared vegetables to the pot and drizzle with the olive oil. Keep stirring and, when the onion has softened, press cancel and deglaze the pot with the white wine and chicken stock.

04 Add the diced chicken and gnocchi to the pot, and stir, separating any bits of the gnocchi that are stuck together.

05 Secure the pressure cooker lid and set the valve to sealing. Pressure cook for 5 minutes, followed by a 5-minute controlled/pulse release (otherwise the starch from the gnocchi will decorate your kitchen walls!).

06 Carefully open the lid and season generously with salt and pepper. Stir in all the remaining ingredients for a delicious and creamy soup, and serve with croutons and a sprinkling of basil leaves.

Flavoured Gnocchi I love it when supermarkets have a deal on seasonal gnocchi, particularly in the summer months when you can get tomato and basil flavour. You can mix and match with any gnocchi flavour in this recipe.

SUPER CREAMY CAULIFLOWER & CORN CHOWDER

SERVES 6

PREP 5 MINS

SAUTE 5 MINS

PRESSURE COOK 8 MINS

RELEASE DR

TOTAL COOK TIME 13 MINS

466 CALS

What are we having for dinner? Soup. Better be the one with the sweetcorn in, says all three of our kids, including our adult son, Kyle. Safe to say it's their favourite comfort soup and it's also a fan favourite since we first made it in the pressure cooker back in 2018.

- 4 shallots
- 2 medium sweet potatoes
- 1 tbsp extra virgin olive oil
- 2 tsp frozen chopped garlic
- 960ml/34fl oz/4 cups cold vegetable stock
- 900g/2lb frozen sweetcorn
- 650g/1½lb frozen cauliflower florets
- 2 × 165g/5¾oz packs cream cheese (we use Philadelphia Light)
- 175g/6oz/1¾ cups grated mature/sharp Cheddar
- 1 tbsp dried oregano
- 1 tbsp dried mixed herbs
- 1 tsp sweet paprika

01 Press sauté and, as the pot warms up, peel and finely slice the shallots, and peel and chop the sweet potatoes into 2cm/¾in chunks. Add the shallots and sweet potatoes to the cooking pot, along with the olive oil, and sauté until the onion has softened.

02 Cancel sauté, add the frozen garlic, and stir. Pour in the stock to deglaze the pot, then stir in the frozen sweetcorn. Place the cauliflower on top of the sweetcorn without stirring.

03 Secure the pressure cooker lid and set the valve to sealing. Pressure cook for 8 minutes, followed by a 10-minute delayed release.

04 Carefully open the lid and season generously with salt and pepper. Stir in the remaining ingredients and serve. (It's okay that the cauliflower breaks down; this adds some nice texture to the soup and lets the sweetcorn be the star.)

White, Red or Sweet? I love this soup for using up the ingredients we have in the kitchen already. You can use sweet, white or red potatoes, keeping the same quantities.

SERVES
6

PREP
8 MINS

SAUTE
5 MINS

PRESSURE COOK
65 MINS

RELEASE
QPR

TOTAL COOK TIME
70 MINS

430 CALS

BITS & BOBS HARISSA SOUP

Do you ever find yourself with bits and bobs in the pantry that you keep meaning to use when you cook, but just haven't got around to yet? This is our go-to 'let's have a spring clean of the store cupboard' kind of soup. Those few butter beans in the bottom of the brown bag, the dried chickpeas that are left over from making some hummus, that harissa paste you forgot you had . . . Add in some fresh vegetables and you have a comforting, hearty soup.

2 large sweet potatoes
3 large carrots
1 medium red onion
140g/5oz/¾ cup dried butter beans/lima beans
1 tbsp chopped frozen garlic
1 tbsp chopped frozen ginger
1 tbsp chopped fresh coriander/cilantro
2 tbsp harissa paste, plus extra to drizzle
1 tbsp sun-dried tomato paste
960ml/34fl oz/4 cups cold vegetable stock
240ml/8½fl oz/1 cup tomato & red pepper sauce (from page 136), or passata

FOR THE CHICKPEAS

175g/6oz/1 cup dried chickpeas
½ tsp harissa paste
½ tsp smoked paprika
1 tbsp extra virgin olive oil

01 Place the chickpeas and 720ml/24⅓fl oz/3 cups cold water in the cooking pot. Secure the pressure cooker lid and set the valve to sealing. Pressure cook for 40 minutes, followed by a quick pressure release. Put the cooked chickpeas to one side in a mixing bowl and drain the liquid from the cooking pot. Add the harissa paste and smoked paprika to the chickpeas and stir to coat in the spices.

02 Meanwhile, peel and dice the sweet potatoes and carrots into medium chunks, and peel and dice the onion.

03 Load all the ingredients apart from the chickpeas and the tomato and red pepper sauce into the cooking pot. Secure the pressure cooker lid and set the valve to sealing. Pressure cook for 25 minutes, followed by a quick pressure release.

04 Carefully open the lid and season generously with salt and pepper. Stir in the tomato and red pepper sauce and three-quarters of the spiced chickpeas and stir well. There's no need to press sauté, as the pot will already be hot.

05 After dishing up the soup, wipe the cooking pot clean, then press sauté. Add the remaining chickpeas and the olive oil, and cook until toasted. Press cancel, then sprinkle the crispy chickpeas on top of the soup, drizzle with a bit more harissa and serve with flatbreads.

TOMATO & RED PEPPER SAUCE

MAKES 4 FREEZER CUBES
PREP 10 MINS
SAUTE 8 MINS
PRESSURE COOK 5 MINS
RELEASE QPR
TOTAL COOK TIME 13 MINS

93 CALS PER CUBE

1 medium red onion
1 red (bell) pepper/capsicum
1 tbsp extra virgin olive oil
1 garlic bulb
650g/1½lb tomatoes
240ml/8floz/1 cup cold vegetable stock
15g/½oz fresh basil leaves
2 tbsp tomato purée/paste
1 tsp Worcestershire sauce
2 tsp dried basil
2 tsp dried oregano
1 tsp granulated sugar

Red pepper and tomatoes, fresh basil and garlic, and very simple to pressure cook.

01 Peel and dice the onion, and deseed and slice the pepper into bite-sized chunks. Add these prepared veg to the cooking pot with the olive oil. Press sauté and, while the pot is warming up, peel and quarter all the garlic cloves and quarter the tomatoes. Sauté the onion and peppers until the onion has softened, then add the garlic and tomatoes, and sauté for about 5 minutes, or until the tomatoes have softened. Press cancel and deglaze the cooking pot with the vegetable stock.

02 Scatter the basil leaves over the top, then secure the pressure cooker lid and set the valve to sealing. Pressure cook for 5 minutes, followed by a quick pressure release.

03 Carefully open the lid and season generously with salt and pepper. Add all the remaining ingredients, then sauté for about 5 minutes to cook out the seasonings, then press cancel and pulse with a stick blender for a smooth tomato and pepper sauce.

GLUTEN-FREE CHEESE SAUCE

MAKES 2 FREEZER CUBES
PREP 8 MINS
SAUTE 5 MINS
PRESSURE COOK 8 MINS
RELEASE QPR
TOTAL COOK TIME 13 MINS

591 CALS PER CUBE

1 large cauliflower, broken into florets
450g/1lb butternut squash, peeled and chopped (prepared weight)
360ml/12fl oz/1½ cups cold veg stock
170g/6oz/1⅔ cups grated mature/sharp Cheddar
⅛ tsp mustard powder
2 tsp dried oregano
1 tsp sweet paprika

Cauliflower, butternut squash and vegetable stock are the base ingredients for this gluten-free cheese sauce.

01 Place the cauliflower florets and the prepared butternut squash in the cooking pot. Pour in the vegetable stock. Secure the pressure cooker lid and set the valve to sealing. Pressure cook for 8 minutes, followed by a quick pressure release.

02 Carefully open the lid and season generously with salt and pepper. Stir in the grated cheese and remaining seasonings. Sauté for about 5 minutes to cook out the spices, then press cancel and pulse with a stick blender for a smooth and creamy cheese sauce.

HIDDEN VEG CURRY SAUCE

MAKES
3 FREEZER CUBES

PREP
8 MINS

SAUTE
5 MINS

PRESSURE COOK
8 MINS

RELEASE
QPR

TOTAL COOK TIME
13 MINS

189 CALS

450g/1lb peeled butternut squash
900g/2lb carrots, peeled and sliced
½ garlic bulb
5cm/2in piece of fresh root ginger
720ml/24⅓fl oz/3 cups cold veg stock
1 tsp curry powder
4 tsp dried coriander/cilantro leaf
2 tsp ground cumin

Butternut squash, carrots, garlic and ginger make the base of this curry sauce.

01 Cut the butternut squash into cubes and place in the cooking pot with the carrots. Peel and roughly chop the garlic cloves and ginger, and add these, too. Pour in the vegetable stock, sprinkle over the curry powder and stir. Secure the pressure cooker lid and set the valve to sealing. Pressure cook for 8 minutes, followed by a quick pressure release.

02 Carefully open the lid and season generously with salt and pepper. Stir in the remaining seasonings and sauté for about 5 minutes to cook out the spices, then press cancel and pulse with a stick blender until you have a smooth and creamy curry sauce.

GREEN GODDESS SAUCE

MAKES
3 FREEZER CUBES

PREP
8 MINS

SAUTE
5 MINS

PRESSURE COOK
8 MINS

RELEASE
QPR

TOTAL COOK TIME
13 MINS

180 CALS PER CUBE

2 medium broccoli
5 celery sticks
1 green (bell) pepper/capsicum
1 medium courgette/zucchini
720ml/24⅓fl oz/3 cups cold veg stock
55g/2oz fresh spinach leaves
250g/9oz/1 cup ricotta cheese
15g/½oz fresh basil leaves
1 tbsp garlic purée
1 tsp dried oregano

Loaded with 6 different greens, add this hidden green veg sauce to pasta or curries, such as our green Thai curry on page 198.

01 Chop the broccoli into medium florets, clean and slice the celery, and deseed and chop the pepper. Cut the courgette into medium slices.

02 Add the prepared vegetables to the cooking pot, pour in the vegetable stock, stir, then cover with the spinach leaves. Secure the pressure cooker lid and set the valve to sealing. Pressure cook for 8 minutes, followed by a quick pressure release.

03 Carefully open the lid and season generously with salt and pepper. Stir in the ricotta, basil leaves, garlic purée and dried oregano. Sauté for about 5 minutes to cook out the seasonings, then press cancel and pulse with a stick blender until you have a smooth and creamy green sauce.

MIREPOIX STARTER BASE CUBES

MAKES 4 FREEZER CUBES
PREP 10 MINS
SAUTE 10 MINS
PRESSURE COOK 5 MINS
RELEASE QPR
TOTAL COOK TIME 15 MINS

121 CALS

- 3 medium brown onions
- 255g/9oz celery sticks
- 900g/2lb carrots
- 1 tbsp extra virgin olive oil
- 960ml/32fl oz/4 cups cold veg stock

Try This Quick Prep Method Our chicken casserole recipe on page 188 could use these cubes. Skip step 1 with this starter base.

This has to be one of the best things of all time to make ahead to help reduce your meal prep time, as so many recipes start with peeling, chopping and sautéing onion, carrots and celery. This flavoursome French cuisine mixture is a base used in a lot of stews, soups and casseroles.

01 Peel and dice the onions, clean and slice the celery, and peel and dice the carrots.

02 Press sauté, place the prepared vegetables in the cooking pot and drizzle in the olive oil. Sauté until the onion has softened.

03 Deglaze the cooking pot with the vegetable stock and continue to cook for about 5 minutes to let the vegetables sweat out in the stock.

04 Cancel sauté, secure the lid and set the valve to sealing. Pressure cook for 5 minutes, followed by a quick pressure release.

05 After releasing the pressure, leave the mixture to cool, then divide into quarters and freeze in freezer cubes.

RED ONION GRAVY

MAKES 2 FREEZER CUBES
PREP 5 MINS
SAUTE 10 MINS
PRESSURE COOK 0 MINS
RELEASE QPR
TOTAL COOK TIME 10 MINS

188 CALS

- 2 large red onions
- 1 tbsp extra virgin olive oil
- 2 tbsp Worcestershire sauce
- 480ml/17fl oz/2 cups cold beef stock
- 1 tbsp plain/all-purpose flour

I make this when I have spare onions. You can use this as a replacement for stock.

01 Peel and cut the onions into long, thin slices. Tip them into the cooking pot and drizzle with the olive oil. Press sauté and cook until softened.

02 Drizzle in the Worcestershire sauce and let the onions sweat for 5 minutes.

03 Cancel sauté, deglaze the cooking pot with the beef stock and give it a good stir. Secure the pressure cooker lid and set the valve to sealing. Pressure cook for 0 minutes, followed by a quick pressure release.

04 Make a paste by mixing the flour with 4 tablespoons water. Carefully open the lid and stir this into the gravy. Press sauté and stir until thickened.

Freezer Gravy I always have a freezer full of frozen gravy cubes. Simply pour unused gravy into silicone cubes and place them in the freezer once cooled. You can use it as gravy or as a stock for flavouring other dishes, like beef stew.

SPEEDY SIDES

HOW TO PRESSURE COOK ANY VEGETABLE

Fun fact: the first food we ever cooked in the pressure cooker was broccoli. After the final beep and releasing the pressure for the first time, my initial thought – apart from how on earth did it cook so fast? – was how is the broccoli so green? Compared to the colour of broccoli when it is boiled in a pan, the pressure-cooked broccoli was so vibrant. It also tasted better – just like organic veg, even though it wasn't. We never boiled another vegetable again!

The method for cooking broccoli, sprouts, cauliflower, carrots and even parsnips is exactly the same. Learn one, alter the time and temp according to which vegetable you are cooking, and you can do them all. Let us show you how it's done with some delicious Brussels sprouts, another beautifully green vegetable.

BRUSSELS SPROUTS

SERVES 4
PREP 10 MIN
SAUTE 0 MINS
PRESSURE COOK 3 MINS
RELEASE QPR
TOTAL COOK TIME 3 MINS

60 CALS

450g/1lb Brussels sprouts, peeled

01 Pour 240ml/8½fl oz/1 cup cold water into the cooking pot. Add the steamer basket and fill it with the sprouts.

02 Secure the pressure cooker lid and set the valve to sealing. Pressure cook for 3 minutes, followed by a quick pressure release.

03 Carefully remove the lid and lift out the steamer basket with the cooked sprouts. Season with salt and pepper and serve.

Cook in the Water vs Steamer Basket I like to think of pressure cooking in the water like boiling in a pan, whereas cooking in a steamer basket is like traditional steaming. Veg cooked in the steamer basket is more flavoursome, whilst veg cooked in water is best suited to big portion sizes.

Vegetables for Soups, Stews & Sauces If you're doing a big batch of veg for soups and stews, it's best to cook them in veg stock in the cooking pot; just make sure you season afterwards not before.

Making Your Vegetables a Meal Follow our vegetable cooking times opposite and pair it with dishes that have a similar cooking time. This is what we've done with the pork chops dinner on page 164 and the peri peri chicken and rice on page 168. If they cook in the same amount of time, you can just add your vegetables to the pot.

DO YOU HATE PEELING A SWEDE?

Swede (also known as rutabaga, turnip or neeps) has a hard skin and can be an effort to peel. Instead, follow this quick peel hack. Pour 240ml/8½fl oz/1 cup of cold water into the cooking pot and place a whole, unpeeled swede on the trivet/rack. Secure the pressure cooker lid and set the valve to sealing. Pressure cook for 8 minutes, followed by a quick pressure release. Wait until it's cool enough to handle, then remove from the pot. The skin will now be super soft and you'll be able to peel it like a sweet potato.

VEGETABLE COOKING TIMES

These times all use quick pressure release, and are based on 240ml/8½fl oz/1 cup cold water in the cooking pot, using a steamer basket or trivet.

Acorn squash, halved 15 minutes
Asparagus 2 minutes
Baby carrots 5 minutes
Beetroot/beet (whole medium) 15 minutes
Broccoli/cauliflower florets 2 minutes
Brussels sprouts 3 minutes
Butternut squash, halved 15 minutes
Butternut squash/pumpkin, cubed 2 minutes
Cabbage, shredded 0 minutes
Carrots, sliced 3 minutes
Frozen broccoli/cauliflower florets 0 minutes
Frozen Brussels sprouts 0 minutes
Frozen peas/sweetcorn 0 minutes
Spaghetti squash, halved 10 minutes
Kale 0 minutes
Leeks, sliced 1 minute
Parsnips, sliced into batons 3 minutes
Potatoes, 3cm/1¼in chunks 10 minutes
Swede/rutabaga, 2cm/¾in cubes 5 minutes
Tenderstem broccoli/broccolini 2 minutes
Turnip, 2cm/¾in cubes 3 minutes

BLANCHING VEG IN THE PRESSURE COOKER FOR FREEZING

These times all use quick pressure release, and are based on 240ml/8½fl oz/1 cup cold water in the cooking pot, using a steamer basket or trivet.

Broccoli florets 0 minutes
Cauliflower florets 0 minutes
Butternut squash, cubed 0 minutes
Brussels sprouts 2 minutes
Carrots, diced 2 minutes

Remove the veg from the pressure cooker and drop into an ice bath. Tip onto a baking tray and freeze, then transfer to freezer bags and label.

MAPLE CHORIZO BRUSSELS SPROUTS

SERVES 4
PREP 5 MINS
SAUTE 5 MINS
PRESSURE COOK 0 MINS
RELEASE N/A
TOTAL COOK TIME 5 MINS

348 CALS

170g/6oz chorizo
55g/2oz/¼ cup salted butter, straight from the fridge
1 tsp dried thyme
450g/1lb just-cooked Brussels sprouts (see recipe page 142)
1 tsp balsamic vinegar
4 tsp maple syrup

Upgrade your just-pressure-cooked Brussels sprouts with chorizo, melted butter and a maple glaze.

01 Press sauté, then cut the chorizo into medium slices and chop each one in half to make half-moons.

02 Add the chorizo to the cooking pot, along with the butter and the thyme. Sauté until the chorizo has softened and the butter has melted. Press cancel. Stir in the sprouts and season with salt and pepper.

03 Transfer the sprouts to a serving dish, drizzle the balsamic vinegar and maple syrup over the top and mix with a serving spoon. Serve warm.

ZERO-MINUTE FROZEN BROCCOLI

SERVES 2
PREP 1 MIN
SAUTE 0 MINS
PRESSURE COOK 0 MINS
RELEASE QPR
TOTAL COOK TIME 0 MINS

96 CALS

450g/1lb frozen broccoli florets
½ medium lemon
2 pinches of chilli flakes

Got some frozen broccoli? Try cooking it from frozen in the pressure cooker.

01 Pour 240ml/8½fl oz/1 cup cold water into the cooking pot. Add the steamer basket and fill it with the frozen broccoli.

02 Secure the pressure cooker lid and set the valve to sealing. Pressure cook for 0 minutes, followed by a quick pressure release.

03 Carefully remove the lid, then lift out the steamer basket. Serve the broccoli with a couple of squeezes of lemon juice, plenty of salt and pepper, and a sprinkling of chilli flakes.

SERVES
6

PREP
8 MINS

SAUTE
4 MINS

PRESSURE COOK
0 MINS

RELEASE
QPR

TOTAL COOK TIME
4 MINS

671 CALS

BROCCOLI & CAULIFLOWER CHEESE

My favourite comfort food from childhood was always what I called a veggie bake. Veggie bakes were basically different vegetables in a cheese sauce - usually cauliflower, broccoli, carrots and whatever else was in season. But my favourites were cauliflower and broccoli. This is how to put together a veggie bake quickly, using your pressure cooker. It is perfect for Sunday dinners and also freezes and reheats well.

1 medium broccoli
1 medium cauliflower
480ml/17fl oz/2 cups cheese sauce (see page 136)
28g/1oz/¼ cup grated mature/sharp Cheddar, for sprinkling

01 Pour 240ml/8½fl oz/1 cup cold water into the cooking pot and add the steamer basket. Break the broccoli and cauliflower into medium-sized florets and add them to the steamer basket.

02 Secure the pressure cooker lid and set the valve to sealing. Pressure cook for 0 minutes, followed by a quick pressure release.

03 Carefully remove the lid, then lift out the steamer basket and set aside. Drain the liquid from the cooking pot.

04 Press sauté and add the cheese sauce to the pot. Stir with a wooden spoon until the cheese sauce is warmed through. Press cancel and return the veg to the cooking pot. Stir to coat in the sauce. Sprinkle with the grated cheese and serve.

MEXICAN STREET CORN

MAKES 4

PREP 5 MINS

SAUTE 0 MINS

PRESSURE COOK 10 MINS

RELEASE QPR

TOTAL COOK TIME 10 MINS

155 CALS

4 corn on the cobs

FOR THE CREMA

1 tbsp salted butter, melted
½ tsp garlic purée
1 heaped tbsp light mayonnaise
1 heaped tbsp sour cream
1 tbsp finely chopped deseeded green jalapeños (adjust to taste)
1 tbsp grated Parmesan
1 tbsp fresh lime juice

TO SERVE

1 spring onion/green onion, sliced
1 tbsp finely chopped fresh coriander/cilantro
1 tbsp finely chopped green jalapeños
1 tbsp grated Parmesan

Your corn on the cob just got a Mexican upgrade. While your corn is pressure cooking, make a delicious creamy topping to load over the corn and transport you to Mexico.

01 Pour 240ml/8½fl oz/1 cup cold water into the cooking pot and add the trivet/rack. Place the corn in a single layer on top.

02 Secure the pressure cooker lid and set the valve to sealing. Pressure cook for 10 minutes, followed by a quick pressure release.

03 In the meantime, make the corn topping. Combine all the crema ingredients in a bowl, mix and set aside.

04 Carefully remove the pressure cooker lid and use tongs to remove the corn. Arrange the cobs on a serving dish. Spoon the crema ingredients over the top, then sprinkle with the spring onion, coriander, jalapeños and Parmesan to serve.

CORN COOKING TIMES

Corn on the cob 10 mins
Corn on the coblettes 4 mins
Frozen corn on the coblettes 10 mins

CARROT & SWEDE MASH

SERVES 4
PREP 10 MINS
SAUTE 0 MINS
PRESSURE COOK 15 MINS
RELEASE QPR
TOTAL COOK TIME 15 MINS

257 CALS

1 large swede/rutabaga
1kg/2lb 4oz medium carrots
360ml/12fl oz/1½ cups cold veg stock
55g/2oz/¼ cup salted butter, softened
1 tsp dried thyme

The Great British Christmas side dish - creamy mashed carrot and swede which is fast to cook but super delicious.

01 Peel and chop the swede and carrots into medium chunks.

02 Pour the stock into the cooking pot and add the steamer basket. Tip the veggies into the steamer basket.

03 Secure the pressure cooker lid and set the valve to sealing. Pressure cook for 15 minutes, followed by a quick pressure release.

04 Carefully remove the lid and lift out the steamer basket. Transfer the veg to a large mixing bowl.

05 Add the butter, thyme and a generous seasoning of salt and pepper to the bowl, then mash the veg with a potato masher until smooth and lump free.

THANKSGIVING BROWN BUTTER RUTABAGA

SERVES 4
PREP 6 MINS
SAUTE 4 MINS
PRESSURE COOK 8 MINS
RELEASE QPR
TOTAL COOK TIME 12 MINS

100 CALS

1 large swede/rutabaga
4 garlic cloves, peeled
2 tbsp salted butter, softened
6 fresh thyme sprigs, leaves picked

Brown Butter This is the process of melting butter until it turns from its natural yellow to a light brown. Hence the name.

This is our American readers' favourite for Thanksgiving. Rutabaga, also known as turnips, neeps or swede, depending on where you live in the world, is delicious pressure cooked, then drizzled with brown butter.

01 Peel and chop the swede into 2cm/¾in cubes and peel the garlic cloves.

02 Pour 240ml/8½fl oz/1 cup cold water into the cooking pot and add the steamer basket. Add the swede chunks and garlic cloves to the basket.

03 Secure the pressure cooker lid and set the valve to sealing. Pressure cook for 8 minutes, followed by a quick pressure release.

04 Carefully remove the lid, lift out the steamer basket and set aside. Drain the liquid from the cooking pot.

05 Add the butter to the cooking pot and press sauté. Once the butter is bubbling, cancel sauté and add the pressure-cooked garlic (it will be mushy). Stir well then add half the thyme leaves. Once the butter has changed colour, quickly remove it from the heat.

06 Tip the swede into a serving dish, season generously with salt and pepper, drizzle over the garlic brown butter and sprinkle over the remaining thyme.

BABY POTATOES (3 WAYS)

I love cooking baby potatoes in the pressure cooker. They are so easy to prep and they cook in an impressive 8 minutes or under. Here are 3 amazing ways to serve them – one for your Sunday roast, one for a summer evening and one for your next curry night in.

GARLIC BUTTER BABY POTATOES

SERVES 4

PREP 6 MINS

SAUTE 2 MINS

PRESSURE COOK 8 MINS

RELEASE QPR

TOTAL COOK TIME 10 MINS

228 CALS

1kg/2lb 4oz baby potatoes, scrubbed
1½ tbsp salted butter, straight from the fridge
4 garlic cloves, minced
2 tbsp roughly chopped fresh parsley

I just love it when we eat out at a restaurant and your side dish is the most amazing baby potatoes, with melted butter and plenty of freshly chopped parsley. This is how to recreate the restaurant classic at home.

01 Pour 240ml/8½fl oz/1 cup cold water into the cooking pot, add the steamer basket and place the baby potatoes inside.

02 Secure the pressure cooker lid and set the valve to sealing. Pressure cook for 8 minutes, followed by a quick pressure release.

03 Carefully remove the lid, lift out the steamer basket and set aside. Pour away the cooking liquid (this would make brilliant vegetable stock for a future recipe so don't throw it away).

04 Press sauté, but set it to a low, as you don't want it to get too hot. Add the butter ½ tablespoon at a time, then the garlic, and sauté, stirring with a wooden spoon, until the butter has melted, then cancel sauté straight away.

05 Tip the baby potatoes into a serving dish, then pour over the butter and garlic, season generously with salt and pepper and sprinkle with parsley.

SERVES
8

PREP
6 MINS

SAUTE
0 MINS

PRESSURE
COOK
4 MINS

RELEASE
QPR

TOTAL
COOK TIME
4 MINS

200 CALS

900g/2lb baby potatoes, scrubbed and halved
3 large eggs
2 tsp garlic powder
¼ tsp smoked paprika

MAYONNAISE DRESSING

4 heaped tbsp full-fat mayonnaise
¼ medium red onion, finely chopped
2 tbsp pickle juice from a jar of pickles or gherkins
1 tsp Dijon mustard

PAPRIKA & MUSTARD POTATO SALAD

Forget cooking the potatoes in one pan and the eggs in another. Everything cooks together in this pressure cooker potato salad. It feeds 8 and is perfect for taking with you to a barbecue or a party, or could just be a nice side dish for the summer. **(See page 153 for a photograph.)**

01 Pour 240ml/8½fl oz/1 cup cold water into the cooking pot, add the steamer basket and place the potatoes inside. Sit the eggs on top of the potatoes.

02 Secure the pressure cooker lid and set the valve to sealing. Pressure cook for 4 minutes, followed by a quick pressure release.

03 Carefully remove the lid and lift out the steamer basket. Place the eggs in a bowl of cold water and set the potatoes aside. When the eggs are cool enough to handle, peel and cut them into wedges.

04 Meanwhile, make the dressing. Add all the ingredients to a medium bowl, mix well and set aside.

05 Once the potatoes have cooled a little, add the potatoes and the egg chunks to the bowl with the dressing. Season generously with salt and pepper and add the garlic powder. Gently mix with a spoon before serving with a sprinkling of paprika.

SERVES
4

PREP
6 MINS

SAUTE
6 MINS

PRESSURE COOK
8 MINS

RELEASE
QPR

TOTAL COOK TIME
14 MINS

205 CALS

1 medium red onion
750g/1½lb baby potatoes, scrubbed
1 tbsp extra virgin olive oil
2 garlic cloves
1 tsp cumin seeds
½ tsp turmeric
1 red chilli
2 tbsp ginger purée
360ml/12fl oz/1½ cups cold vegetable stock
1 tbsp Greek yoghurt
1 tsp garam masala
2 tsp tomato purée/paste
½ tsp ground coriander
175g/6oz fresh spinach leaves

CURRY NIGHT IN SAAG ALOO

My go-to at any Indian restaurant is always a saag aloo. It's a delicious side dish loaded with Indian flavours, potatoes and spinach. It's so easy to recreate at home, though, so why not have a curry night in and this can be your hero side dish. You can see it photographed on page 73 with our lamb curry and mushroom rice.

01 Peel and dice the red onion, and halve or quarter the baby potatoes, depending on their size.

02 Press sauté and add the chopped onion and potatoes to the pot, with the olive oil. Sauté until the onion has softened.

03 Meanwhile, thinly slice the garlic cloves, then add to the pot with the cumin seeds and turmeric. Finely slice and deseed the chilli, then add to the pot, too. Cancel sauté, then stir in the ginger purée and deglaze the pot with the vegetable stock.

04 Give everything one last stir, then secure the pressure cooker lid and set the valve to sealing. Pressure cook for 8 minutes, followed by a quick pressure release.

05 Carefully remove the lid and press sauté. Stir in the remaining ingredients and continue to cook until the spinach has wilted. (The potatoes should be nice and fork tender.)

LET'S STACK DINNER

STACKED MEALS

It was 2019 when we stacked a meal for the first time. We were making spaghetti Bolognese (see page 176). We loved this efficient, no-stir meal, where all the ingredients were stacked on top of each other. There were layers of onion and mince, spaghetti, then the pasta sauce. After cooking, a quick stir led to a delicious pot of spaghetti Bolognese. That was our first attempt and it made us hungry for more. In this chapter we've put together all our favourite recipes that use the stacking method.

WHAT IS STACKING?

Stacking is where you stack multiple foods on top of one another. Either in containers, such as steamer baskets and springform tins/pans, or directly on top of each other.

WHY STACK?

It makes cooking times quicker and stops your food going cold. Instead of cooking your mashed potatoes separately to your meatloaf, you can cook it all together in one cooking pot.

WHICH ORDER SHOULD YOU STACK THE FOOD?

You will see mashed potatoes stacked above in our bangers and mash on page 162, yet it is below in our meatloaf and mashed potatoes on page 160. Confused? Well, it's all about what works best with that particular recipe. The food that cooks most slowly generally goes at the bottom in the liquid and cooking up top is good for slowing food down. But you can only cook food in the bottom that pressure cooks well in liquid. For example, meatloaf is wrapped in foil, so it wouldn't work well in the liquid. Whereas seabass would cook too quickly in the liquid. Meanwhile, the veg served with these needs liquid, so should be cooked below.

THE MOST IMPORTANT LESSON TO REMEMBER WITH STACKING

Pair ingredients with similar cooking times, or include a food that won't spoil if it's cooked for longer than it needs. Throughout this book we've listed many cooking times; simply browse for ingredients with similar cooking times and create your own stackable meals.

THE 3 MAIN TYPES OF STACKED FOOD

Cooking Pot & Steamer Basket This is where we cook one food in the cooking pot and another in the steamer basket. We use this method with recipes like bangers and mash. Mash is a brilliant part of a stackable meal because if it cooks for a couple of minutes extra it won't spoil.

Cooking Pot & Food On The Rack This is very similar to cooking in a steamer basket, but instead of a basket, you're using your trivet/rack. Because the trivet has holes in it, you can add a layer of foil or make a foil parcel and place it on top.

Individual Ingredients Stacked This is where you stack ingredients on top of each other without stirring. It's like magic when the food is stirred at the end. Chicken fajitas is one of the recipes made this way, and works because taking the peppers out of the liquid and placing them on the trivet slows down the cooking. Whereas mushroom rice takes the oven-baked rice method to the pressure cooker, where the rice and liquids are in the bottom of the cooking pot and the mushrooms sit on top.

WHAT IS POT IN POT COOKING?

Pot in pot cooking, often abbreviated to PIP, is when you use a separate cooking container inside the cooking pot.

PIP first became popular for stacking meals because it allowed you to cook food in the main cooking pot whilst cooking another kind of food above, such as cooking potatoes or rice at the same time as a protein.

One of the reasons PIP is often used in pressure cooking is because the food is kept out of the main liquid and so cooks more slowly, which makes it perfect for delicate foods like salmon.

Any container that is pressure cooker friendly can sit on the trivet/rack to create a pot in pot experience. Or you can use foil-wrapped parcels, like the meatloaf photographed here, to achieve the same results.

Our favourites containers include: ceramics, such as ramekins or little casserole dishes that fit the shape of your cooking pot; and glassware, such as Pyrex. Silicone is also pressure-cooker friendly. We use this for our egg loaf on page 28. Another great option are freezer cubes – you can use silicone freezer cubes in the pressure cooker on the trivet/rack to reheat food. Stainless steel is extremely popular, too, such as a springform tin/pan for a cheesecake, a pudding basin for your Christmas pudding, or a small round cake tin for when you're making rice.

How to Cook the PIP Way

01 Pour the liquid into the cooking pot

02 Add the trivet or rack

03 Add the food in its container

04 Secure the lid and start pressure cooking

SERVES
6

PREP
15 MINS

SAUTE
0 MINS

PRESSURE COOK
25 MINS

RELEASE
DR

TOTAL COOK TIME
25 MINS

776 CALS

1 small brown onion
900g/2lb minced/ground beef
2 tsp garlic purée
2 tsp tomato purée/paste
2 large eggs
55g/2oz/1 cup fresh breadcrumbs
1 tbsp Worcestershire sauce
2 tsp dried parsley
1 tbsp dried oregano
1 tbsp sweet paprika
1 tsp mustard powder
2 tbsp tomato ketchup

MASHED POTATOES

1.35kg/3lb white potatoes
480ml/17fl oz/2 cups cold vegetable stock
125g/4½oz/generous ½ cup salted butter
1 tbsp dried parsley
2 tbsp whole/full-fat milk

MEATLOAF & MASHED POTATOES

The potato chunks cook directly in the cooking pot, whilst the meatloaf cooks on the rack above. It's easy and a time saver. As the meatloaf rests, you can mash the potatoes and everything will be ready at the same time.

01 Prepare the meatloaf. Peel and finely slice the onion and place in a mixing bowl. Add all the remaining meatloaf ingredients, except the ketchup, and mix well with your hands. (Alternatively, if you don't like having onion texture in meatloaf, you can blend the ingredients in a food processor.) Form into a big loaf shape.

02 Place a long piece of foil on the work surface (about 30cm/12in long). Wrap the meatloaf tightly in the foil. Make sure there is crease/join at the top so it's easy to open. You can prep this ahead and chill in the fridge for later.

03 Peel and dice the potatoes and load them into the bottom of the cooking pot. Pour in the stock, then add the tall trivet/rack over the potatoes. Gently place the foil-wrapped meatloaf on the trivet.

04 Secure the pressure cooker lid and set the valve to sealing. Pressure cook for 25 minutes, followed by a 5-minute delayed pressure release.

05 Open the lid and carefully remove the trivet and meatloaf. Set it aside to rest.

06 Drain the potatoes and transfer them to a mixing bowl. Add the butter, season generously with salt and pepper, and sprinkle in the dried parsley. Mash the potatoes, then gradually add the milk until you have a smooth, creamy mash.

07 Open up the foil parcel to reveal the meatloaf and smother the top with the tomato ketchup.

08 Slice the meatloaf and serve with the mashed potatoes, gravy and kale.

SERVES
4

PREP
5 MINS

SAUTE
5 MINS

PRESSURE COOK
8 MINS

RELEASE
QPR

TOTAL COOK TIME
13 MINS

866 CALS

BANGERS & MASH

This is another example of how you can cook two foods at once by stacking. With bangers and mash, we do the opposite of the meatloaf and mash. We cook the sausages in the stock and the mash above. We served our bangers and mash with the red onion gravy from page 139.

- 1 tbsp extra virgin olive oil
- 8 sausages (we use Cumberland)
- 480ml/17fl oz/2 cups cold beef stock
- 1.35kg/3lb white potatoes
- 125g/4½oz/generous ½ cup salted butter
- 1 tbsp dried thyme
- 2 tbsp whole/full-fat milk

01 Press sauté. Drizzle the olive oil into the cooking pot and add the sausages, spreading them out so they don't overlap. Sauté until the sausages are brown to your liking. Turn them for an even colouring. Press cancel.

02 Pour the beef stock over the sausages and deglaze the pot. Add the steamer basket over the sausages. Peel and dice the potatoes, then load them into the basket.

03 Secure the pressure cooker lid and set the valve to sealing. Pressure cook for 8 minutes, followed by a quick pressure release.

04 Remove the steamer basket and transfer the potatoes to a mixing bowl. Add the butter and season generously with salt and pepper, and the dried thyme. Mash the potatoes, then gradually add the milk until you have a smooth, creamy mash.

05 Serve the bangers with the mashed potatoes, peas and onion gravy (see page 139).

Reusing Stock As we served our bangers and mash with our freezer cubes onion gravy, we didn't need the beef stock from the cooking pot. There's no need to discard it, though – save it for another recipe!

SERVES
1

PREP
8 MINS

SAUTE
0 MINS

PRESSURE COOK
10 MINS

RELEASE
QPR

TOTAL COOK TIME
10 MINS

848 CALS

225g/8oz baby potatoes, scrubbed
2 medium carrots
115g/4oz Brussels sprouts
300ml/10½fl oz/1¼ cups cold vegetable stock
2 tsp salted butter
1 pork chop (2cm/¾in thick)
¼ tsp dried rosemary
¼ tsp dried thyme
1 tsp apple sauce
1 tbsp finely chopped fresh parsley

THE PORK CHOPS STACK

Have you ever wondered if you can stack your meat, potatoes and two veg in the pot all at once to use your cooking pot for a full meal? This does exactly that with a pork chop, baby potatoes, carrots and sprouts.

01 Place the baby potatoes in the cooking pot. If there are any large potatoes, you can chop them in half. Peel the carrots, then cut them into 2.5cm/1in slices. Halve these slices to make half-moons. Trim and clean the sprouts, then add the carrots and sprouts to the cooking pot with the potatoes.

02 Pour in the vegetable stock, then dot with the butter. Add the tall trivet/rack and cover in foil (so the ingredients won't slip through).

03 Add the pork chop to the foil. Sprinkle over the rosemary and thyme, some salt and pepper, and spoon over the apple sauce.

04 Secure the pressure cooker lid and set the valve to sealing. Pressure cook for 10 minutes, followed by a quick pressure release.

05 Open the lid, season everything generously with salt and pepper, then serve with the parsley sprinkled over the veg.

Swap the Chops Love lamb chops more than pork chops? Simply swap the chops and swap the apple sauce for mint sauce, whilst keeping the same cooking times.

5-MINUTE CHICKEN FAJITAS

MAKES 10

PREP 10 MINS

SAUTE 0 MINS

PRESSURE COOK 5 MINS

RELEASE QPR

TOTAL COOK TIME 5 MINS

365 CALS

30g/1oz fajita seasoning
2 tsp garlic purée
1.2kg/2lb 8oz skinless and boneless chicken thighs or drumsticks
4 (bell) peppers/capsicum (any colour combo)
1 large red onion
1 × 300g/10½oz jar salsa dip

TO SERVE

1 avocado, sliced
2 jalapeños, sliced
1 lime, cut into wedges
1 × 200g/7oz carton sour cream dip
10 mini tortilla wraps

One of the greatest things about pressure cooking chicken is how tender the chicken is and how easily it pulls apart. Making it perfect for chicken fajitas. No sauteing, just stacking everything and letting the pressure cooker work its magic!

01 Pour 360ml/12fl oz/1½ cups cold water into the cooking pot. Add 1 tablespoon of the fajita seasoning and the garlic purée. Stir into the water.

02 Season the chicken generously with salt and pepper and half the remaining fajita seasoning. Add the chicken to the cooking pot, but don't stir. They will be partly submerged in the seasoned water.

03 Deseed the peppers and slice them lengthways. Peel and slice the onion lengthways, too. Scatter them over the chicken, then sprinkle the remaining fajita seasoning over the top, making sure the peppers are not directly in the liquid.

04 Secure the pressure cooker lid and set the valve to sealing. Pressure cook for 5 minutes, followed by a quick pressure release.

05 Open the lid and drain the liquid from the cooking pot. (You could reserve the liquid to use as stock another day.)

06 Using meat claws or a knife and fork, shred the chicken. it will be really tender so it won't require much effort!

07 Stir half the salsa dip into the chicken and vegetables in the pot.

08 Now let's make a chicken fajitas sharing board! Serve the chicken with the remaining salsa, some sliced avocado, jalapeños, lime wedges, sour cream dip and tortilla wraps alongside.

SERVES
4

PREP
5 MINS

SAUTE
5 MINS

PRESSURE COOK
3 MINS

RELEASE
NPR

TOTAL COOK TIME
8 MINS

450 CALS

PERI PERI CHICKEN THIGHS & SPICY RICE

This is a wonderful stacking time saver. Spicy rice cooks in the cooking pot, whilst the marinated chicken thighs cook on the trivet/rack above.

600g/1½lb skinless and boneless chicken thighs
2 tbsp roughly chopped fresh coriander/cilantro, to serve
Lime wedges, to serve

MARINADE

2 tsp each smoked paprika, garlic powder, dried oregano and dried coriander/cilantro leaf
4 tsp soft brown sugar
1 tbsp extra virgin olive oil
1 tbsp fresh lime juice
1 tbsp peri peri sauce (we use Nando's medium), plus extra to serve

SPICY RICE

1 medium red onion
1 red (bell) pepper/capsicum
1 tbsp extra virgin olive oil
2 tsp peri peri sauce, adjust to taste (we use Nando's medium)
200g/7oz/1 cup white basmati rice, rinsed
½–1 tsp turmeric
160g/5¾oz/1 cup frozen peas
1 tsp garlic powder
1 tsp dried oregano

01 Place the marinade ingredients in a large bowl. Mix well, then add the chicken and mix again. Cover the bowl with cling film/plastic wrap and leave to marinate in the fridge for a couple of hours, or overnight, if possible.

02 To make the spicy rice, peel and dice the onion, deseed and dice the pepper. Add them to the cooking pot with the olive oil and sauté until the pepper has softened. Press cancel.

03 Pour 360ml/12fl oz/1½ cups cold water into the pot and deglaze. Add the peri peri sauce to the water and mix well. Stir in the rice and the turmeric.

04 Add the trivet/rack to the pot over the rice and place a layer of foil on top, followed by the marinated chicken thighs.

05 Secure the pressure cooker lid and set the valve to sealing. Pressure cook for 3 minutes, followed by a full natural pressure release.

06 Open the lid and remove the trivet/rack with the chicken and set aside.

07 Add the frozen peas to the rice, a generous seasoning of salt and pepper, and the garlic powder and oregano. If it's not yellow enough, adjust with a little extra turmeric. Give the rice a good stir and serve with the chicken, some more peri peri sauce, some fresh coriander and lime wedges.

Spice Level This recipe is mildly spiced. If you prefer it without spice, omit the peri peri. If you like it hotter, add an extra 2 teaspoons peri peri to the cooked rice and stir.

Reheating Chicken & Rice Load some leftovers into a casserole dish that fits in your cooking pot. Pour 240ml/8½fl oz/1 cup cold water into the cooking pot, then add the trivet/rack and place your casserole dish on top. Secure the lid and set the valve to sealing. Pressure cook for 5 minutes, followed by a quick pressure release. Stir and it's ready for eating.

Peri Peri Wraps Love going out for a chicken and rice wrap? Use your leftovers and add 2 tablespoons peri peri mayonnaise, mix it up and load into wraps with shredded lettuce and sliced tomatoes.

SERVES
4

PREP
5 MINS

SAUTE
3 MINS

PRESSURE COOK
0 MINS

RELEASE
QPR

TOTAL COOK TIME
3 MINS

410 CALS

- 1kg/2lb 4oz minced/ground chicken
- 2 tbsp extra virgin olive oil
- 3 tbsp soy sauce
- 1 tbsp rice vinegar
- 1 tsp ground ginger
- 1 tsp garlic powder
- 120ml/4fl oz/½ cup cold chicken stock
- 2 × 300g/10½oz bags coleslaw mix (raw cabbage, onion and carrot)
- 1 tsp Chinese five spice
- 4 tsp teriyaki sauce
- 1 spring/green onion, sliced

EGG ROLL IN A BOWL

Not heard of an egg roll in a bowl before? It's a fun Chinese dish where you combine the ingredients you'd normally find inside an egg roll or a spring roll, then serve it in a bowl. It's also quick prep because this classic pressure cooker recipe uses coleslaw mix, rather than individually chopped veg.

01 Place the chicken mince in the cooking pot, along with the olive oil, then press sauté. Use a wooden spoon to break up the chicken as the pot warms up.

02 Cancel the sauté when the chicken is three quarters cooked. Pour in the soy sauce and rice vinegar, and add the ginger and garlic, too. Pour in the cold chicken stock and give it all a good stir. Finally, sprinkle the coleslaw mix over the chicken but don't stir.

03 Secure the pressure cooker and set the valve to sealing. Pressure cook for 0 minutes, followed by a quick pressure release.

04 Open the lid, add the Chinese 5 spice and season generously with salt and pepper. Give it a good stir.

05 Transfer to bowls, then drizzle with a little teriyaki sauce and sprinkle over the sliced spring onion.

SERVES
2

PREP
6 MINS

SAUTE
3 MINS

PRESSURE COOK
5 MINS

RELEASE
DR

TOTAL COOK TIME
8 MINS

511 CALS

THE SEABASS STACK

Seabass, baby potatoes, green beans and mangetout. Plus, a creamy parsley sauce. All in one cooking pot.

- 225g/8oz baby potatoes, scrubbed
- 240ml/8½fl oz/1 cup cold fish stock
- 1½ tbsp salted butter
- 2 x 115g/4oz seabass fillets, skin on
- 2 tsp fish seasoning (see page 79)
- 85g/3oz green beans
- 85g/3oz mangetout
- 1½ tbsp roughly chopped fresh parsley
- 2 tbsp dry white wine
- 2 slices of lemon
- 3 heaped tbsp crème fraîche

01 Halve the baby potatoes, keeping any miniature ones whole. Place the potatoes in the cooking pot, then pour in the fish stock, and dot with half the butter.

02 Add the tall trivet/rack to the pot over the potatoes and season the seabass with a sprinkling of fish seasoning. Place a large layer of foil on the work surface to use as a foil packet for your seabass and veg. Arrange the green beans and mangetout, the seabass, half the chopped parsley, the remaining butter, the wine and slices of lemon on the foil. Wrap the foil around the seabass and veg to create a foil parcel.

03 Place the foil parcel on the trivet. Secure the pressure cooker lid and set the valve to sealing. Pressure cook for 5 minutes, followed by a 3-minute delayed pressure release.

04 Open the lid and remove the trivet with the foil packet. Scoop out the baby potatoes, leaving just 4 tablespoons of the cooking liquid in the pot.

05 Divide the potatoes between 2 plates, then unwrap the parcels and add the veg and seabass to the plates, too. Drizzle the liquid from the foil packets into the cooking pot. Press sauté, then add in the crème fraîche and sauté until you have a creamy sauce. Press cancel, add in the remaining parsley, then pour the sauce over the seabass and veg to serve.

SERVES
4

PREP
5 MINS

SAUTE
2 MINS

PRESSURE COOK
3 MINS

RELEASE
DR

TOTAL COOK TIME
5 MINS

300 CALS

5-MINUTE MUSHROOM RICE

Later in this chapter (on page 178) we teach you how to make beef stroganoff using a triple stacking technique. This is the double version – think of it as a practice run.

55g/2oz/¼ cup salted butter, straight from the fridge
2 tsp garlic purée
1 tbsp fresh thyme leaves
325g/11½oz chestnut mushrooms
360ml/12fl oz/1½ cups cold vegetable stock
200g/7oz/1 cup white basmati rice, rinsed

01 Press sauté and add the butter. Sauté until the butter has melted, then press cancel. Quickly take the pot off the heat as you don't want it to burn.

02 Stir in the garlic purée and add half the thyme. Chop large mushrooms into quarters, halve medium ones and keep the small ones whole. Add the mushrooms to the pot and coat them well in the garlic butter. Transfer the garlic butter mushrooms to a bowl.

03 Pour the vegetable stock into the pot to deglaze it, scraping any bits from the bottom of the pan. Tip in the rice, stir, then place all the garlic mushrooms over the rice. Don't stir anymore, as you want to create layers of mushrooms and rice.

04 Secure the pressure cooker lid and set the valve to sealing. Pressure cook for 3 minutes, followed by a 10-minute delayed pressure release.

05 Open the lid and season generously with salt and pepper. Stir the rice and mushrooms to combine, then transfer to a serving dish. Sprinkle with the remaining thyme and serve.

Any Baked Rice If you are new to kitchen gadget cookery, then this recipe is like baked rice, where everything is stacked and bakes together in the oven. Follow the liquid ratios and cooking times and do the same with your other favourites.

SERVES 6

PREP 5 MINS

SAUTE 6 MINS

PRESSURE COOK 5 MINS

RELEASE QPR

TOTAL COOK TIME 11 MINS

510 CALS

1 medium brown onion
1 tbsp extra virgin olive oil
750g/1lb 10oz minced/ground beef
720ml/24⅓fl oz/3 cups cold beef stock
200g/7oz dried spaghetti
500g/1lb 2oz pasta sauce
1 tbsp garlic purée
1 tbsp tomato purée/paste
1 tbsp dried oregano
3 tbsp roughly chopped fresh basil, plus extra to serve
2 tbsp grated Parmesan, to serve

SPAGHETTI BOLOGNESE

This was the first pressure cooker stacking meal that we fell in love with and it's still a favourite seven years later. Bolognese, then spaghetti, then pasta sauce - all stacked before pressure cooking. Once done, stir and you have a big pot of spag bol.

01 Press sauté. Peel and finely chop the onion, then tip into the cooking pot with the olive oil. Leave it to sizzle, then stir until the onion has softened.

02 Add the mince and break down with a wooden spoon as you brown it on all sides – but don't fully cook the mince, as the pressure cooker will do this. Press cancel.

03 Deglaze the pot with the beef stock and give it a good stir. Break the spaghetti into thirds then add to the pot over the meat, spreading the small pieces of spaghetti out, as you don't want it sticking together. Pour the pasta sauce over the spaghetti, spreading it out as you pour. Finally, half fill the pasta sauce jar with water, cover with a lid and shake it to make sure any bits stuck to the side come loose, then pour this over, too. (It's important your spaghetti is well covered so you don't get dry bits.)

04 Secure the pressure cooker lid and set the valve to sealing. Pressure cook for 5 minutes, followed by a quick pressure release.

05 Open the lid and it will look like spaghetti soup. This is fine as it thickens as you stir. Add the purées, the oregano, chopped basil and a generous seasoning of salt and pepper, then stir for a couple of minutes, until thickened.

06 Serve with a sprinkling of Parmesan and extra basil.

SERVES
6

PREP
10 MINS

SAUTE
5 MINS

PRESSURE COOK
3 MINS

RELEASE
QPR

TOTAL COOK TIME
8 MINS

621 CALS

CREAMY BEEF STROGANOFF WITH TAGLIATELLE

Kyle says this is the best recipe I have ever made in the pressure cooker. He always jokingly tells me it needs extra testing, just so I make it again for him. It's a stacking miracle. Just think of the non-gadget effort - cooking mushrooms, making the sauce, a separate pan for pasta . . . Yet here it is, all in one pot cooked together.

1 medium brown onion
2 × 225g/8oz rump/sirloin steaks
200g/7oz button mushrooms
1 tbsp extra virgin olive oil
480ml/17fl oz/2 cups cold beef stock
2 tsp Worcestershire sauce
240ml/8½fl oz/1 cup red wine
2 tsp mustard powder
4 tsp smoked paprika
4 tsp dried dill
8 nests dried tagliatelle
55g/2oz/¼ cup salted butter, straight from the fridge
1 × 280g/10oz pack cream cheese (we use full-fat Philadelphia)
Roughly chopped fresh parsley, to serve

01 Peel and slice the onion, and slice the rump steaks into strips. Halve or quarter the mushrooms, depending on their size, or keep them whole if they are small.

02 Press sauté and drizzle the olive oil into the cooking pot. When it warms up, add the onion and sauté until softened, then add the steak and brown on all sides.

03 Cancel the sauté, and deglaze the pot with the stock. Make sure you use a silicone spatula or wooden spoon to get any bits that are stuck to the bottom of the pot. Add the Worcestershire sauce, the wine, half the mustard powder, paprika and dill, and stir. Place the pasta on top, making sure most of the pasta is submerged to stop it drying out. Cover the pasta with the mushrooms and dot with the butter.

04 Secure the pressure cooker lid and set the valve to sealing. Pressure cook for 3 minutes, followed by a quick pressure release.

05 Open the lid and stir. Add the cream cheese, the remaining seasonings and a generous seasoning of salt and pepper. Keep stirring for 1–2 minutes. The heat from pressure cooking will soften the cheese, so there's no need to put it back on sauté.

06 Leave the stroganoff to sit in the cooking pot for a couple of minutes to thicken before serving sprinkled with the parsley.

COOK ONCE, EAT TWICE

COOK ONCE, EAT TWICE

I tried freezer meals once. It was the beginning of 2017 when freezer meals and pressure cooking were the best things since sliced bread. I spent half a day making 20 meals with Dom, freezing them, then using the pressure cooker to reheat them. Although the meals were okay, there was no wow factor. Pressure cooking is so fast that losing half a day to meal prep didn't excite me.

However, something else did . . . the thought of cooking once but eating twice. The idea is to make more food than you need, then freeze the bits and bobs you have left. You're then building up a portfolio of freezer meals for later – and freezer meals without spending half a day making them!

The other plus point of cooking once and eating twice versus freezer meals is that often the frozen food is already cooked. So, you don't have to worry about thin liquids when reheating, or blanching potatoes before freezing.

HOW DO YOU DO IT?

If you're new to this concept, think of how you've gradually built up what was an empty pantry when you moved into your first place. Perhaps you bought a couple more cans of baked beans than you needed . . . Your pantry soon grew and it was handy to have this quick supply for when you didn't have time to go shopping.

Cooking once and eating twice is similar; you make more mash than you're going to eat for dinner, then freeze what's left. You double up on your Bolognese and the leftovers head to the freezer. Do this just 2 times a week and you have 2 freezer meals a week. Over the course of a month, that makes 8 meals, which means a full week without having to cook! Over the pages that follow, we have a delicious variety of recipes you can double up on.

Serving Sizes Many of the recipes in this chapter are for feeding four people. If you're only feeding one, then you can add three portions to the freezer! If you're cooking for two, you'll add two.

Freezer Cubes The ones we have used the most in this chapter are a 500ml/18fl oz/2 cup quantity. If you are using them with potatoes and veg, then one cube will feed two people, otherwise assume one cube per person.

REHEATING MINCE (2 WAYS)

Straight In the Cooking Pot Method Place 120ml/4fl oz/½ cup cold water in the cooking pot. Add the frozen freezer cube of mince to the water. Secure the pressure cooker lid and set the valve to sealing. Pressure cook for 10 minutes, followed by a quick pressure release. Finish with a 2-minute sauté to break up any tiny frozen bites and to give it a good mix.

Pot In Pot Method Place 240ml/8½fl oz/1 cup cold water in the cooking pot and place the trivet/rack inside. Arrange the frozen freezer cube of mince in a container, then place the container on the trivet. You can use a stainless steel, ceramic or even glass container. Continue as above but cook for 30 minutes instead. It's longer because the food is in a container and not directly in the pot.

Which Method Should You Use? The general rule is that if they hold liquid, e.g. savoury mince, stocks, soups and stews, you can cook them directly in the cooking pot. But if it has a thick texture, such as corn chowder or mashed potatoes, it is likely to burn to the cooking pot and is better suited to pot in pot reheating. Foods that might be ruined by being cooked in a little water are also best pot in pot.

MAKES
3

PREP
5 MINS

SAUTE
8 MINS

PRESSURE COOK
5 MINS

RELEASE
QPR

TOTAL COOK TIME
13 MINS

MIX & MATCH MINCE FREEZER CUBES

Wouldn't it be nice to open the freezer and have some different freezer cubes to choose from, instead of just feeling like everything is the same? Let us show you how to cook the mince, then use it as a base for sloppy Joes, keema or a savoury mince for your next cottage pie. So, here's a master recipe and the extra ingredients to transform it into 3 different meals. You can double the quantities in this recipe and make enough for 6 freezer cubes. Keep the same cooking times. Or perhaps just make 3 batches of your favourite mince – triple the quantities of the flavourings, if you're going to do that. Just make the recipe work for you.

MASTER INGREDIENTS

1 medium brown onion
1 tbsp extra virgin olive oil
1kg/2lb 4oz minced/ground beef (5% fat)
120ml/4fl oz/½ cup cold beef stock
500g/1lb 2oz/2 cups passata
2 tsp beef gravy granules

SLOPPY JOES

1 tbsp Worcestershire sauce
60ml/2fl oz/¼ cup tomato ketchup
1 tbsp tomato purée/paste
1 tsp dried oregano
1 tsp smoked paprika

KEEMA

80g/3oz/½ cup frozen peas
1 tsp each garlic purée, ginger purée and tomato purée/paste
2 tsp each garam masala, ground cumin and ground coriander
2 pinches–¼ tsp chilli flakes (adjust to taste)
Finely chopped fresh coriander/cilantro

SAVOURY MINCE

3 medium carrots
80g/3oz/½ cup frozen peas
1 tsp dried thyme
1 tsp dried parsley

01 Press sauté on the pressure cooker. Peel and dice the onion. Peel and thinly slice the carrots (for the savoury mince), then chop them in half to make half-moons. Add the onion to the cooking pot along with the olive oil, then start sauteing.

02 Once the onion has started to soften, add the minced beef and continue to sauté until the mince is three-quarters cooked. Press cancel. Add the beef stock, give it a stir, then pour the passata over the mince but don't stir.

03 Because the carrots are just for the savoury mince, we cook them separately to make meal prep easier. Place a trivet/rack lined with foil over the mince and passata, then line with the carrots.

04 Secure the pressure cooker lid and set the valve to sealing. Pressure cook for 5 minutes, followed by a quick pressure release.

05 Open the lid and remove the trivet with the carrots and place to one side. Stir the gravy granules into the pot to help thicken the liquid, and season generously with salt and pepper. This is your master beef recipe.

06 Place two thirds to one side and focus on batch 1. Depending on which you want for dinner, why not make that one last so it's warm and ready to eat when you finish, while your supplies for the freezer are cooling ready to be frozen?

07 For the Sloppy Joes, just add the Worcestershire sauce, tomato ketchup, oregano and paprika to the mince, and give it a stir. This will fill one 500ml/18fl oz/2 cups quantity freezer cube.

08 For the keema, stir in the frozen peas, purées and spices. Finish with a sprinkling of finely chopped coriander. This will fill one 500ml/18fl oz/2 cup quantity freezer cube.

09 For the savoury mince, stir in the cooked carrots, frozen peas, dried thyme and parsley. This will fill one 500ml/18fl oz/2 cup quantity freezer cube.

SERVES
8

PREP
8 MINS

SAUTE
0 MINS

PRESSURE COOK
8 MINS

RELEASE
QPR

TOTAL COOK TIME
8 MINS

548 CALS

3kg/6lb 8oz white potatoes
480ml/17fl oz/2 cups cold vegetable stock
225g/8oz/1 cup salted butter
2 heaped tbsp garlic cream cheese (we use garlic Philadelphia)
4 tsp dried parsley

8-MINUTE MASHED POTATOES

We love mashed potatoes, but they can feel time consuming to make. You'll love this fast-cooking version with an extra creamy secret ingredient. Plus, leftovers can go into your freezer cubes.

01 Peel and chop the potatoes into medium chunks.

02 Pour the stock into the cooking pot and add the steamer basket. Tip the potatoes into the basket, then dot with half the butter.

03 Secure the pressure cooker lid and set the valve to sealing. Pressure cook for 8 minutes, followed by a quick pressure release.

04 Remove the steamer basket with the potatoes and transfer them to a large mixing bowl. Add the remaining butter, the cream cheese, parsley and a generous seasoning of salt and pepper. Mash with a potato masher until smooth and lump free.

05 Serve, or leave to cool and spoon into freezer cubes.

MAKES
8

PREP
5 MINS

SAUTE
0 MINS

PRESSURE COOK
45 MINS

RELEASE
QPR

TOTAL COOK TIME
45 MINS

218 CALS

8 medium baking potatoes

FREEZER JACKET POTATOES

Make a big batch of jacket/baked potatoes, have some for dinner and freeze the rest!

01 Using a fork, prick your potatoes so that the steam can escape.

02 Pour 240ml/8½fl oz/1 cup cold water into the cooking pot and add the steamer basket. Arrange the potatoes in the steamer basket.

03 Secure the pressure cooker lid and set the valve to sealing. Pressure cook for 45 minutes, followed by a quick pressure release. (If your potatoes are large, increase the cooking time to 60 minutes.)

04 Open the lid and 8 potatoes are ready. Have 4 now and freeze the rest!

To Freeze Arrange the potatoes on a large plate. Place the plate in the freezer for 2 hours, then remove and transfer the potatoes to a freezer bag. This stops them sticking together and makes it easy to grab them one at a time from the freezer.

Reheating Frozen Jackets Follow steps 2 and 3 above to reheat from frozen, but pressure cook for 25 minutes instead of 45 minutes. You'll have piping hot potatoes ready for dinner in almost half the time.

SERVES 8

PREP 12 MINS

SAUTE 8 MINS

PRESSURE COOK 6 MINS

RELEASE CR/QPR

TOTAL COOK TIME 14 MINS

480 CALS

- 720ml/24⅓fl oz/3 cups cold beef stock
- 1.8kg/4lb white potatoes, peeled and roughly chopped
- 55g/2oz/¼ cup salted butter
- 80g/3oz/½ cup frozen peas
- 85g/3oz tenderstem broccoli/broccolini
- 150g/5½oz garlic and herb cream cheese (we use Boursin)
- 2 tsp Dijon mustard
- Lingonberry jam, to serve

SWEDISH MEATBALLS

- 50g/1¾oz/1 cup fresh breadcrumbs
- 2 shallots, finely chopped
- 2 tbsp whole/full-fat milk
- 325g/11½oz minced/ground beef
- 250g/9oz minced/ground pork
- 1 large egg
- 2 tsp garlic purée
- 1 tsp mustard powder
- ½ tsp ground allspice
- ½ tsp ground nutmeg
- 2 tsp dried parsley

SWEDISH MEATBALLS & MASH

No butter, no cream and no flour in this delicious Swedish meatball recipe.

01 Pour the beef stock into the cooking pot, then add the potatoes too.

02 To make the meatballs, add all the ingredients to a mixing bowl. Mix with your hands, then form the mixture into 24 balls, about the size of a table tennis ball.

03 Add the trivet/rack to the cooking pot and place it over the potatoes. Arrange 12 of the meatballs on a large flat plate and place in the freezer. Place the remaining 12 meatballs on the trivet. Secure the pressure cooker lid and set the valve to sealing. Pressure cook for 4 minutes, followed by a 6-minute controlled/pulse pressure release.

04 Open the lid and carefully lift out the trivet and meatballs. Set aside.

05 Transfer the potatoes to a mixing bowl. Add the butter and 1 tablespoon of the cooking liquid, plus a generous seasoning of salt and pepper. Mash with a potato masher until smooth. Transfer half the mash to silicone freezer cubes and place in the freezer once cool.

06 Meanwhile, place a steamer basket in the cooking pot and add the peas and broccolini. Secure the pressure cooker lid and set the valve to sealing. Pressure cook for 2 minutes, followed by a quick pressure release.

07 Open the lid and remove the steamer basket and broccolini. Pour half the beef stock from the cooking pot into silicone freezer cubes (like the mash).

08 Press sauté and wait for the remaining beef stock to warm up. Tip the cream cheese into the cooking pot. Add 2 heaped tablespoons of the mash, to thicken the sauce, as well as the Dijon mustard. Stir with a wooden spoon to create a creamy sauce. Press cancel, then return the cooked meatballs to the sauce and stir well.

09 Serve the meatballs with the mash, sauce, peas, broccolini and jam.

To Freeze Once the remaining uncooked meatballs on the plate are frozen, transfer them to a freezer bag, then return to the freezer. (By placing them on a plate first, it stops them sticking together in the freezer.) The cubes of stock should also be in the freezer, as well as the cubes of mash. You now have enough beef stock, mashed potatoes and uncooked meatballs for next time!

Reheating Your Leftovers Defrost the leftover stock and mashed potatoes. Pour the stock into the cooking pot and add the frozen meatballs. Place the tall trivet/rack over the meatballs and add the mash to a silicone pan and place on the trivet. Close the lid and set the valve to sealing. Pressure cook for 5 minutes, followed by a quick pressure release. Load the mash and meatballs onto plates, then use the heat from the pot to mix a tub of Boursin and 2 teaspoons Dijon with the stock. Stir to make a creamy gravy. Pour over to serve.

SERVES 6

PREP 10 MINS

SAUTE 5 MINS

PRESSURE COOK 15 MINS

RELEASE QPR

TOTAL COOK TIME 20 MINS

617 CALS

CHICKEN CASSEROLE WITH FENNEL & THYME DUMPLINGS

This is a delicious chicken casserole recipe that can be the master recipe for several things. It's perfect for cooking once and eating twice, and adds some variety to your pressure cooker meals. You can keep it as a simple chicken casserole, add dumplings to it, or use as the filling for pies.

1 medium brown onion
5 celery sticks
4 large carrots
1 tbsp extra virgin olive oil
960ml/32fl oz/4 cups cold chicken stock
4 medium red potatoes
600g/1lb 5oz skinless and boneless chicken breast, diced
2 tsp fresh thyme leaves
2 tsp fennel seeds
320g/11½oz/2 cups frozen peas
150ml/5fl oz/generous ½ cup crème fraîche

FENNEL & THYME DUMPLINGS

175g/6oz/1⅓ cups self-raising/self-rising flour
2 tbsp salted butter
2 tsp fresh thyme leaves
2 tsp fennel seeds
1 large egg
4 tbsp whole/full-fat milk

01 Peel and chop the onion, celery and carrots into bite-sized chunks. Place them in the cooking pot with the olive oil and sauté until the onion has softened. Press cancel, then deglaze the pot with the stock. (You could use a defrosted mirepoix cube instead of this step – see page 139.)

02 Peel and chop the potatoes into medium chunks and add them to the pot, along with the diced chicken. Stir, then set aside.

03 To make the dumpling, add the flour and butter to a bowl. Rub the butter into the flour with your fingertips until it resembles coarse breadcrumbs. Season with salt and pepper, then add the thyme and fennel. Crack in the egg and mix with a fork, then gradually add the milk until the dough comes together. Knead the dough until soft.

04 Shape the dough into dumplings and place them over the casserole. Secure the pressure cooker lid and set the valve to sealing. Pressure cook for 15 minutes, followed by a quick pressure release. (Or you can add the dumplings after pressure cooking the casserole, if you have an air fryer lid – just pop them on top and air fry for 10 minutes at 200°C/400°F.)

05 Remove the lid and stir in the thyme and fennel seeds, and season with salt and pepper. Add the frozen peas and crème fraîche, stir and serve.

You Can Freeze Dumplings
Arrange raw or cooked dumplings on a plate, then place in the freezer until almost frozen. Transfer from the plate to a freezer bag and label. You can then cook them with leftover casserole from frozen.

Chicken & Dumplings Freezer Cubes In order to cook once and eat twice, place half the cooked chicken filling in freezer cubes, leave it to cool, then cover each cube with a dumpling, and freeze. The dumpling will cook as you warm up the filling. These are a perfect for one and a great way to make use of the leftovers.

Casserole In a Bag To reheat, add 240ml/8½fl oz/1 cup cold vegetable stock to the cooking pot, then take the frozen casserole out of the bag and place in the stock. It will sink down as it goes to pressure. Secure the lid and set the valve to sealing. Pressure cook for 8 minutes, followed by a quick pressure release. Stir, then add the raw dumplings on top and pressure cook again for 3 minutes with another quick release.

SUNDAY BEEF BOURGUIGNON

SERVES 6
PREP 12 MINS
SAUTE 8 MINS
PRESSURE COOK 45 MINS
RELEASE DR
TOTAL COOK TIME 53 MINS

400 CALS

Beef bourguignon takes me back to trips to France in the Bordeaux region. It is a delicious beef stew with the perfect amount of red wine and plenty of simple everyday ingredients. Because the cooking time doesn't change from making a pot of stew for 2 as it does for 8, it is a great dish for the cook once, eat twice chapter. I love to serve this with lots of crusty French bread.

- 900g/2lb beef braising/chuck steak
- 3 tbsp salted butter, straight from the fridge
- 4 rashers streaky bacon
- 1 medium red onion
- 5 garlic cloves
- 360ml/12fl oz/1½ cups red wine
- 240ml/8½fl oz/1 cup cold beef stock
- 4 large carrots
- Bouquet garni (we use thyme, rosemary and bay)
- 350g/12oz chestnut mushrooms
- 2 tsp beef gravy granules
- 1 tbsp dried oregano
- 1 tbsp dried thyme
- Fresh thyme, to serve

01 Chop the beef into medium chunks and add them to the cooking pot with 2 tablespoons of the butter. Press sauté and brown on all sides.

02 Remove the meat with tongs and set aside, leaving the butter in the pot. Chop the bacon into bite-sized pieces, and peel and dice the onion. Add these to the pot and sauté until the onion has softened. Peel and roughly chop the garlic and add this, too. Continue to sauté for a couple of minutes, then press cancel.

03 Deglaze the cooking pot with the red wine and stock. Peel and slice the carrots into half-moons, then add them to the pot. Return the meat to the pot and stir. Add the bouquet garni and place the mushrooms on top, but don't stir. (As mushrooms can vary a lot in size, quarter any big ones, halve any medium ones and keep the small ones whole.) Dot the remaining butter over the mushrooms.

04 Secure the pressure cooker lid and set the valve to sealing. Pressure cook for 45 minutes, followed by a 5-minute delayed release.

05 Open the lid, remove the bouquet garni and stir in the gravy granules. Season with the dried oregano and thyme and some salt and pepper. Serve with a sprinkling of fresh thyme.

Cook Once, Eat Twice We've deliberately made this recipe big enough to serve 6. If you save at least 2 of the portions, you can turn your casserole into an old-fashioned suet pudding – see page 192.

Time to Pressure Do note that large pots of stew and soup take the longest time to pressure before the cooking process begins, so expect to wait 15–20 minutes. See our time to pressure test on page 13.

SERVES
4

PREP
15 MINS

SAUTE
0 MINS

PRESSURE COOK
1 HOUR

RELEASE
NPR

TOTAL COOK TIME
1 HOUR

811 CALS

Olive oil spray, for greasing

2 portions of Sunday dinner beef Bourguignon (see page 190)

SUET PASTRY

225g/8oz/1⅔ cups self-raising/self-rising flour

100g/3½oz/scant ⅔ cup shredded suet (we use Atora)

MONDAY NIGHT BEEF BOURGUIGNON PUDDING

We couldn't do a pressure cooker book without everyone's favourite old-fashioned pudding. A stew-like filling plus suet pastry - forget a 5-hour cooking time and using string, this sits on your trivet/rack and is cooked in 1 hour. But it can still be time consuming making the filling, making the pastry and, of course, assembling it . . . So, I had an idea . . . What if you use stew or casserole leftovers? Then you just need to make your pastry, load it up and pressure cook! Setting aside 2 portions of our beef Bourguignon from page 190, we are taking the cook once, eat twice to a whole new level with this pressure cooker pudding.

01 To make the pastry, tip the flour and suet into a mixing bowl, season with salt and pepper, and pour in 5 tablespoons cold water. Mix the dough, gradually adding a little more water, if necessary, until you have a dough consistency. We found that 8 tablespoons cold water in total was perfect. Knead the dough for a few minutes, until soft.

02 Spray a pudding basin with olive oil, then use your hands to grease the base and sides. Roll out two-thirds of the dough and use this to line the base and sides of your basin. Trim off the overhang, then roll the remaining dough to the size of the top of the basin and set aside.

03 Add the leftover beef Bourguignon to the lined basin, loading it up to just over three-quarters full. Don't be tempted to overfill it. Place the reserved dough on top of the basin, then add a layer of foil.

04 Place the low trivet/rack in the cooking pot (you want the steamed pudding as low down as possible in the pressure cooker), then top with the foil-covered basin. Carefully pour boiling water down the sides of the pot, until the water comes about a quarter of the way up the sides of the basin.

05 Secure the pressure cooker lid and set the valve to sealing. Pressure cook for 1 hour, followed by a full natural pressure release.

06 Open the lid and carefully remove the steamed pudding. Set it aside to cool a little, then remove the foil and flip it over onto a serving dish. Let it rest and, as it cools, it will release from the basin. Slice into it and watch the filling gush out before serving.

Double Up & Freeze You can make a double batch of the pastry and freeze half for another time. Roll it into a dough ball and transfer to a freezer bag.

BEEF SHIN PUDDING

SERVES 4

PREP 15 MINS

SAUTE 8 MINS

PRESSURE COOK 1 HOUR 45 MINS

RELEASE DR/NPR

TOTAL COOK TIME 1 HOUR 53 MINS

695 CALS

650g/1lb 7oz beef shin
1 tbsp extra virgin olive oil
1 medium brown onion
2 garlic cloves
240ml/8½fl oz/1 cup red wine
120ml/4fl oz/½ cup cold beef stock
Olive oil spray, for greasing
1 tbsp Worcestershire sauce
4 tsp tomato purée/paste
2 tsp beef gravy granules

SUET PASTRY

225g/8oz/1⅔ cups self-raising/self-rising flour
100g/3½oz/scant ⅔ cup shredded suet (we use Atora)

Whilst my go-to is to make a savoury pudding from stew leftovers, I also love beef shin, which just falls apart when pressure cooked, is so flavoursome and makes a delicious steamed pudding filling.

01 Chop the beef shin into chunks and remove all visible fat. Place the meat in the cooking pot, drizzle over the olive oil and press sauté. Brown the beef on all sides. As it's browning, peel and thinly slice the onion and garlic. Remove the meat with tongs and set aside. Add the onion and garlic to the pot and sauté until the onion has softened. Press cancel, then deglaze the pot with the red wine and beef stock.

02 Return the meat to the pot, secure the pressure cooker lid and set the valve to sealing. Pressure cook for 45 minutes, followed by a 5-minute delayed release.

03 Meanwhile, to make the pastry, tip the flour and suet into a mixing bowl, season with salt and pepper, and pour in 5 tablespoons cold water. Mix the dough, gradually adding a little more water, if necessary, until you have a dough consistency. We found that 8 tablespoons cold water in total was perfect. Knead the dough for a few minutes, until soft.

04 Spray a pudding basin with olive oil, then use your hands to grease the base and sides. Roll out two-thirds of the dough and use this to line the base and sides of your basin. Trim off the overhang, then roll the remaining dough to the size of the top of the basin and set aside.

05 Open the lid of the cooking pot, add the Worcestershire sauce, tomato purée and a good seasoning of salt and pepper to the beef, then press sauté and add the gravy granules. Stir until thickened.

06 Add the filling to the dough-lined basin, loading it to just over three-quarters full. (Don't be tempted to overfill – put any extra in freezer cubes for another day!) Place the reserved dough on top of the basin, then add a layer of foil.

07 Place the low trivet/rack in the pot (you want the steamed pudding as low as possible in the pressure cooker), then top with the foil-covered basin. Carefully pour boiling water down the sides of the pot, until the water comes about a quarter of the way up the sides of the basin. (There's no need to clean the pot first, so long as you've removed the filling.)

08 Secure the pressure cooker lid and set the valve to sealing. Pressure cook for 1 hour, followed by a full natural pressure release.

09 Open the lid and carefully remove the pudding. Set it aside to cool a little, then remove the foil and flip it over onto a serving dish. Let it rest and, as it cools, it will release from the basin. Slice into it and serve.

SERVES
6

PREP
10 MINS

SAUTE
8 MINS

PRESSURE COOK
8 MINS

RELEASE
QPR

TOTAL COOK TIME
16 MINS

615 CALS

EASY PEASY FISH PIE

The pressure cooker is a brilliant gadget for fish pie. You can use the sauté for the prawns and leeks and for making the sauce. Then you use the pressure cooker for the mashed potatoes and the fish.

MASHED POTATOES

1.35kg/3lb white potatoes
240ml/8½fl oz/1 cup cold vegetable stock
55g/2oz/¼ cup salted butter
2 tsp dried dill

FISH FILLING

1 medium leek
2 tsp extra virgin olive oil
240ml/8½fl oz/1 cup cold fish stock
1kg/2lb 4oz mixed fish pie filling (we use salmon, smoked fish and white fish)
160g/5¾oz/1 cup frozen peas
160g/5¾oz/1 cup frozen sweetcorn
250g/9oz raw super king prawns/shrimp
2 tsp fresh lemon juice
2 tsp dried dill
2 tsp dried parsley
2 tsp dried chives

01 Peel and chop the potatoes into medium chunks. Pour the vegetable stock into the cooking pot and add the steamer basket, then tip the potatoes into the basket. Secure the pressure cooker lid and set the valve to sealing. Pressure cook for 8 minutes, followed by a quick pressure release. Open the lid and carefully remove the steamer basket and the potatoes, and transfer them to a large mixing bowl. Discard the liquid in the pot.

02 Clean and thinly slice the leek, add it to the pot along with the olive oil. Press sauté and cook until the leeks are starting to get some colour to them. Press cancel, then deglaze the pot with the fish stock. Add the fish and stir. Secure the pressure cooker lid and set the valve to sealing. Pressure cook for 0 minutes, followed by a quick pressure release.

03 Meanwhile, add the butter and dried dill to the potatoes, and season generously with salt and pepper. Mash with a potato masher until smooth and lump free. Set aside.

04 Open the lid of the pressure cooker and stir in the frozen peas, sweetcorn and prawns. Press sauté and sauté until the prawns are a beautiful shade of pink, then press cancel.

05 Stir 2 heaped tablespoons of mashed potatoes into the fish filling. This thickens the sauce brilliantly. Season again with some salt and pepper, add the lemon juice, dried dill, parsley and chives, and stir one last time.

06 Top with the mashed potato and serve with rocket/arugula leaves and lemon wedges.

Air Fryer Lid If your cooker has an air fryer lid, you can place the mash over the cooked fish pie filling and air fry for 8 minutes at 200°C/400°F for a crusty topping (as shown opposite).

Cook Now, Eat Twice We placed leftover fish pie filling in freezer cubes and placed leftover mash in some others. That way, we could mix and match for our next dinner. We could turn the leftovers into another serving of fish pie, or use the mash for something else, and have the fish pie filling with rice.

SERVES
6

PREP
10 MINS

SAUTE
6 MINS

PRESSURE COOK
2 MINS

RELEASE
QPR

TOTAL COOK TIME
8 MINS

273 CALS

GREEN THAI CURRY

This is a great example of cooking once, eating twice. Green Thai curry can be rather thin and it's hard to get the colour right and achieve a creamy curry base. What we do differently here is use our green goddess sauce from page 137, which has hidden green vegetables, and serve it with another 3 vegetables in the curry. It makes a great healthy dish to cook again and again.

360g/12¾oz asparagus
360g/12¾oz green beans
520g/1lb 2½oz baby corn
1 quantity green goddess sauce (see page 137)
4 tsp each garlic purée, ginger purée and lemongrass paste
2 tbsp Thai green curry paste (adjust to taste)
2 tsp fish sauce
1 x 400g/14oz can coconut milk
Thai basil leaves, to serve
Lime wedges, to serve

01 Pour 240ml/8½fl oz/1 cup cold water into the cooking pot and add the steamer basket. Remove the woody ends from the asparagus and trim the green beans. Add all the veg to the steamer basket.

02 Secure the pressure cooker lid and set the valve to sealing. Pressure cook for 2 minutes, followed by a quick pressure release.

03 Open the lid, lift the steamer basket out and discard the cooking liquid. Press sauté and add the green goddess sauce to the pot along with the garlic and ginger purées, the lemongrass and Thai green curry pastes, and the fish sauce.

04 Once it has started to bubble away and is coming together nicely, press cancel and stir in the coconut milk. Finish by returning the vegetables to the pot and stirring again. Serve over brown rice with lime wedges and a squeeze or two of lime juice, with Thai basil leaves sprinkled over the top.

Portion Size This curry is enough for 4, or 6 with rice. It's a perfect recipe to make for 2 people tonight, then freeze the leftovers for 2 or 4 for another day.

SWEET TREATS

NOT ANOTHER PRESSURE COOKER CHEESECAKE

If you've visited any social media platform in order to learn about pressure cooking, the chances are that you've seen loads of cheesecakes. They are top of the bucket list of things to make and the reason why you should get a pressure cooker. But, before you think to yourself, 'Not another cheesecake!', hear me out. Making a baked-style cheesecake in a pressure cooker is a true wow moment. The result is just like a baked cheesecake but it's so smooth, and the recipe is easy to mix and match with other flavours.

SERVES
8

PREP
10 MINS

SAUTE
0 MINS

PRESSURE COOK
30 MINS

RELEASE
NPR

TOTAL COOK TIME
30 MINS

390 CALS

100g/3½oz digestive biscuits/ graham crackers
28g/1oz/⅛ cup unsalted butter, melted
3 × 165g/6oz packs cream cheese (we use full-fat Philadelphia)
200g/7oz/1 cup granulated sugar
2 large eggs
1 tbsp vanilla extract
5 heaped tbsp sour cream

VANILLA CHEESECAKE

This is our cheesecake master recipe. Master this first, then turn the page for some delicious fruity toppings.

01 Tip the biscuits into a bowl and use the end of a rolling pin to bash them to crumbs. Pour the melted butter into the bowl and mix well until combined.

02 Tip the biscuit mixture into a springform tin/pan (our tin is 18cm/7in). Press the mixture down with the back of a spoon or a spatula until level. Place in the freezer to set for 20 minutes whilst you make your filling.

03 Place the cream cheese and sugar in a large mixing bowl and mix with an electric hand mixer until super creamy and well combined. Crack in the eggs one at a time, mixing after each addition, then add the vanilla and keep mixing. Finally add the sour cream, and you should now have a creamy cheesecake batter. Pour the mixture over the biscuit base, levelling it with the back of a spoon. Cover the tin with foil.

04 Pour 360ml/12fl oz/1½ cups cold water into the cooking pot, then add the trivet/rack. Lower the cheesecake carefully onto the trivet. Secure the pressure cooker lid and set the valve to sealing. Pressure cook for 30 minutes, followed by a full natural pressure release.

05 Open the lid, but leave the cheesecake to cool in the cooking pot. When it is cool, lift it out, remove the foil and leave it to rest in the fridge overnight.

Always Use the Foil Wrapping the top of the tin loosely with foil stops steam from sneaking in as it pressure cooks.

STRAWBERRY COULIS

SERVES 8
PREP 5 MINS
SAUTE 5 MINS
PRESSURE COOK 0 MINS
RELEASE N/A
TOTAL COOK TIME 5 MINS

92 CALS

325g/11½oz strawberries
60g/2¼oz/½ cup icing/confectioners' sugar
Juice of 1 lemon
140g/5oz/½ cup raspberry jam/jelly

The best way to serve cheesecake is to add some strawberries and turn it into a summer bake for wowing family and friends.

01 Press sauté.

02 Quarter the strawberries and add them to the cooking pot. Add the icing sugar, lemon juice and jam, and continue to sauté until the strawberries have softened and are breaking down. (You can blend partially to make a strawberry sauce or keep them whole.) Press cancel.

03 Spoon the strawberry coulis onto the centre of your cooled cheesecake (see page 202) and let it drip down the edges. Slice and serve with more delicious coulis spooned over the top.

BLACK FOREST & CREAM

SERVES 8
PREP 5 MINS
SAUTE 5 MINS
PRESSURE COOK 0 MINS
RELEASE N/A
TOTAL COOK TIME 5 MINS

300 CALS

325g/11½oz/2 cups frozen black forest fruit mix
4 tbsp granulated sugar
1 tbsp vanilla extract
140g/5oz/½ cup blackberry jam/jelly
300ml/10fl oz/1¼ cups double/heavy cream
2 tsp icing/confectioners' sugar
115g/4oz cherries
½ chocolate flake

My favourite gateau topping but for your cheesecake.

01 Press sauté. Add the frozen fruit, sugar, vanilla and 80ml/2½fl oz/⅓ cup cold water to the cooking pot. Keep stirring and sautéing until the fruit is defrosted and softened. Press cancel.

02 Stir in the jam and leave to cool.

03 Meanwhile, whip the double cream with the icing sugar in a bowl using an electric hand whisk, until thick.

04 Pour the fruit topping over the cheesecake, keeping a 2.5cm/1in gap around the edges. Using a piping/pastry bag, pipe the cream in circles around the edge of the cheesecake. Place a cherry on top of each cream circle, then finish by crumbling the flake over the black forest sauce and the cream.

SERVES
6

PREP
10 MINS

SAUTE
20 MINS

PRESSURE COOK
1 HR 30 MINS

RELEASE
NPR

TOTAL COOK TIME
1 HR
50 MINS

660 CALS

NUT-FREE CHRISTMAS PUDDING

Delicious Christmas pudding cooked in the pressure cooker. Much quicker than the old-fashioned pan method and it can be made ahead, with or without alcohol.

Olive oil spray, for greasing
300g/10½oz dried mixed fruit
50g/1¾oz candied orange peel
75g/2¾oz/¾ cup shredded suet (we use Atora)
100g/3½oz/½ cup soft brown sugar
½ tsp ground nutmeg
½ tsp mixed spice
½ tsp ground ginger
Zest and juice of 1 tangerine
2 large eggs
2 tbsp liquid (we use brandy, milk or stout)
100g/3½oz/¾ cup self-raising/self-rising flour

BRANDY SAUCE

55g/2oz/¼ cup unsalted butter
55g/2oz/scant ½ cup plain/all-purpose flour
600ml/21fl oz/1 pint whole/full-fat milk
4 tbsp brandy
55g/2oz/¼ cup granulated sugar

01 Grease a pudding basin with olive oil and set aside.

02 In a mixing bowl, combine the dried mixed fruit, orange peel, suet, brown sugar and spices. Give it a good stir with a wooden spoon. Add the tangerine zest and juice and the eggs. Give it a good mix. Add in whatever liquid you have chosen – if using milk and keeping it alcohol free, it will only last 2–3 days when cooked. If using brandy or stout, it will last much longer. Stir in the flour and you are now pressure cooker ready.

03 Tip the mixture into the prepared pudding basin, levelling the top with a wooden spoon. Add a layer of foil to the top of the basin. (This will stop the steam from going into your pudding and making it watery.)

04 Place the pudding basin on the trivet/rack with handles, as this will make it easier to get it in and out of the cooking pot. Place the trivet and the pudding basin in the cooking pot. Pour cold water down the side of the pot, until it reaches a quarter of the way up the side of the basin.

05 Secure the pressure cooker lid and set the valve to sealing. Pressure cook for 1 hour 30 minutes, followed by a full natural pressure release.

06 Open the lid and leave until cool enough to handle, then remove the pudding from the cooking pot, remove the foil and set aside to cool fully before removing from the pudding basin.

07 Meanwhile, to make the brandy sauce, press sauté and add the butter. When the butter has melted, stir in the flour, then gradually add the milk to create a creamy sauce. Stir continuously, bringing the sauce to a boil. Leave it to simmer for about 15 minutes, then add the brandy and sugar. Stir again, press cancel, then serve with your Christmas pudding.

Ingredient Hack At Christmas time, many bakeries and health food shops sell a 'bake your own' Christmas cake with the ingredients all weighed out. It is often much cheaper than buying everything separately, and the ingredients are very similar for Christmas pudding. I often get these kits and use the mixed fruit, sugar and seasoning from it to make my pudding.

CAKE BITES (3 WAYS)

In the egg chapter, we showed you lots of different ways to use your egg bite moulds for breakfast and brunch. What you might not know is that you can also use the moulds to satisfy your sweet tooth. Here are 3 delicious ways to turn your favourite mug cake or cake into an egg bite treat.

MAKES
7

PREP
5 MINS

SAUTE
0 MINS

PRESSURE COOK
12 MINS

RELEASE
QPR

TOTAL COOK TIME
12 MINS

191 CALS

- 3 tbsp smooth Biscoff spread, softened
- 1 large egg
- 4 tbsp granulated sugar
- 3 tbsp extra virgin olive oil, plus extra for greasing
- 3 tbsp whole/full-fat milk
- 3 tbsp plain/all-purpose flour

BISCOFF TOPPING

- 2 tbsp smooth Biscoff spread, softened
- 2 Biscoff biscuits/cookies

BISCOFF MUG CAKE BITES

Your favourite Biscoff mug cake made in your egg bite mould. These are perfect for parties, taking on road trips or just for your sweet tooth fix in the fridge.

01 Pour 240ml/8½fl oz/1 cup cold water into the cooking pot, and add the trivet/rack. Grease each of the 7 holes of the egg bite mould with a little olive oil to stop it sticking.

02 Place the Biscoff spread in a mixing bowl, crack in the egg and mix with an electric hand mixer. Gradually add in the sugar, mixing all the time, then the olive oil and milk. Slowly add the flour, then give it one last mix.

03 Divide the batter between the 7 egg bite holes. Cover with the lid and place it gently on the trivet.

04 Secure the pressure cooker lid and set the valve to sealing. Pressure cook for 12 minutes, followed by a quick pressure release.

05 Carefully remove the mould from the cooking pot, then remove the lid and set aside the cake bites to cool.

06 Loosen the edges of the cake bites with the tip of a round-bladed knife, if necessary. Place a dinner plate over the bites, then flip the mould over. Leave the mould upside down over the plate for a couple of minutes and the cake bites will start to drop out on their own. Gently squeeze any that haven't fallen out. But it's a game of patience – if you rush, they will come out like rice pudding!

07 Drizzle Biscoff spread over the tops of the cakes, then break up the biscuits and sprinkle the crumbs over the cakes.

MAKES
14

PREP
10 MINS

SAUTE
0 MINS

PRESSURE COOK
12 MINS

RELEASE
QPR

TOTAL COOK TIME
12 MINS

250 CALS

CHOCOLATE CAKE BITES

Many years ago, when we got our first pressure cooker, I converted my trusted chocolate cake recipe into chocolate cake bites. They were amazing and we made them over and over again. They have the texture of a steamed chocolate pudding but with the flavour of a chocolate cake. (See the photo on page 210.)

- Olive oil spray, for greasing
- 115g/4oz/½ cup unsalted butter, softened
- 225g/8oz/1 heaped cup granulated sugar
- 2 large eggs
- 2 tsp vanilla extract
- 2 tsp extra virgin olive oil, plus extra for greasing
- 28g/1oz/¼ cup unsweetened cocoa powder
- 300ml/10½fl oz/1¼ cups skimmed/fat-free milk
- 200g/7oz/1½ cups self-raising/self-rising flour

CHOCOLATE TOPPING

- 4 tbsp chocolate sauce
- 2 small chocolate flakes

01 Pour 240ml/8½fl oz/1 cup cold water into the cooking pot, and add the trivet/rack. Grease each of the 7 holes of the egg bite mould with a little olive oil to stop it sticking.

02 Place the butter and sugar in a mixing bowl and, using an electric hand mixer, whisk until soft and fluffy. Crack in the eggs, add the vanilla and olive oil, and continue to mix. Next, add the cocoa powder and the milk, and continue mixing. Tip in the flour, then mix slowly with a wooden spoon until combined. (Note: this quantity will make 2 batches of the egg bites.)

03 Divide half the mixture between the 7 egg bite holes. Cover the mould with its lid, then place it gently on the trivet. Secure the pressure cooker lid and set the valve to sealing. Pressure cook for 12 minutes, followed by a quick pressure release.

04 Carefully remove the mould from the cooking pot, then remove the lid and set aside the chocolate cake bites to cool.

05 Loosen the edges of the cake bites with the tip of a round-bladed knife, if necessary. Place a dinner plate over the bites, then flip the mould over. Leave the mould upside down over the plate for a couple of minutes and the cake bites will start to drop out on their own. Gently squeeze any that haven't fallen out. But it's a game of patience – if you rush, they will come out like rice pudding!

06 Repeat with the remaining mixture to make 14 cake bites.

07 Drizzle the tops of the cooled cake bites with the chocolate sauce, then break up the chocolate flakes and sprinkle the crumbs over the cakes.

MAKES
7

PREP
10 MINS

SAUTE
0 MINS

PRESSURE COOK
12 MINS

RELEASE
QPR

TOTAL COOK TIME
12 MINS

597 CALS

250g/9oz/1 cup Greek yoghurt
4 tbsp extra virgin olive oil, plus extra for greasing
2 tsp vanilla extract
Zest and juice of 4 large lemons
2 large eggs
75g/2¾oz/⅓ cup unsalted butter, melted
300g/10½oz/1½ cups granulated sugar
300g/10½oz/2 cups self-raising/self-rising flour

LEMON DRIZZLE
105g/3½oz/¾ cup icing/confectioners' sugar
1 tbsp fresh lemon juice

LEMON DRIZZLE CAKE BITES

Imagine your favourite lemon drizzle cake as a cake bite! These are so delicious and you'll want to go back for seconds.

01 Pour 240ml/8½fl oz/1 cup cold water into the cooking pot, and add your trivet/rack. Grease each of the 7 holes of the egg bite mould with a little olive oil to stop it sticking.

02 Add the Greek yoghurt, olive oil, vanilla extract and lemon juice to a mixing bowl. Crack in the eggs and mix with an electric hand mixer. Pour in the melted butter and mix again, then add most of the lemon zest (save some to decorate the lemon bites later). Add the sugar and mix again, then gradually mix in the flour.

03 Divide the batter between the 7 egg bite holes. Cover with the lid place it gently on the trivet.

04 Secure the pressure cooker lid and set the valve to sealing. Pressure cook for 12 minutes, followed by a quick pressure release.

05 Carefully remove the mould from the cooking pot, then remove the lid and set aside to cool.

06 Loosen the edges of the cake bites with the tip of a round-bladed knife, if necessary. Place a dinner plate over the bites, then flip the mould over. Leave the mould upside down over the plate for a couple of minutes and the cake bites will start to drop out on their own. Gently squeeze any that haven't fallen out. But it's a game of patience – if you rush, they will come out like apple crumble!

07 To make the drizzle, mix the icing sugar with 1–3 teaspoons lemon juice until you have a lump-free mixture. (One teaspoon for a really thick icing or 3 for a thinner mixture.) Spoon the icing over the bites, allowing it to dribble down the sides. Finally, top with some of the reserved lemon zest for the traditional lemon drizzle look.

Get Creative These are just 3 delicious sweet cake bites you can make at home in your pressure cooker. You could do the same with brownie batter for brownie bites, or carrot cake batter for carrot cake bites – try it with any other favourite cake batter, or even try it with banana bread!

DOM'S RICE PUDDING

SERVES
4

PREP
5 MINS

SAUTE
4 MINS

PRESSURE
COOK
12 MINS

RELEASE
NPR

TOTAL
COOK TIME
16 MINS

553 CALS

- 900ml/31fl oz/3¾ cups whole/full-fat milk
- 150g/5½oz/¾ cup granulated sugar
- 200g/7oz/scant 1 cup pudding rice
- 2 tsp vanilla extract
- 28g/1 oz/⅛ cup unsalted butter
- 4 tbsp single/half and half cream

Deliciously sweet rice pudding - this is a trip back to childhood and is so easy to make in the pressure cooker. Don't forget to serve it with your favourite jam.

01 Add the milk, sugar and pudding rice to the cooking pot and press sauté. Stir continuously until it is just coming to the boil. Press cancel.

02 Secure the pressure cooker lid and set the valve to sealing. Pressure cook for 12 minutes, followed by a full natural pressure release.

03 Open the lid, add the vanilla and dot with the butter. Stir until the butter has melted, then pour in the cream. (You won't need to turn the sauté on, as the residual heat from the pressure cooking is enough.)

04 Stir one last time, then serve with your favourite jam/preserve.

Rice Pudding Rice When we lived in Portugal, we couldn't get pudding rice so we used arborio rice instead. It's a great swap if you can't find it either.

DULCE DE LECHE CARAMEL

SERVES
4

PREP
2 MINS

SAUTE
0 MINS

PRESSURE
COOK
35 MINS

RELEASE
QPR

TOTAL
COOK TIME
35 MINS

312 CALS

- 1 x 397g/14oz can sweetened condensed milk

Cold Or Hot Water? You must add cold water to the cooking pot, or it will get to pressure too quickly, and the caramel will be very light, like melted white chocolate.

During the 13 years we spent living in Portugal, we fell in love with *doce de leite*, as it's called there, where it is often used in desserts. It takes several hours to make in a pan on the stove but, in the pressure cooker it's just 35 minutes! You could also save them unopened in your pantry and have dulce de leche ready to go.

01 Remove the label from the condensed milk can. Place the can unopened in the cooking pot. Pour in enough cold water to cover the can (in our 5.7-litre/6-quart cooker it was 2.9 litres/3 quarts).

02 Secure the pressure cooker lid and set the valve to sealing. Pressure cook for 35 minutes, followed by a quick pressure release. (For light, creamy caramel cook for 30 minutes, or for really dark, old-fashioned caramel try 40 minutes.)

03 Open the lid and drain away the water. Use oven gloves or similar to remove the can from the pot and transfer to a bowl of cold water, until cool enough to handle.

04 Open the can, stir and enjoy with your favourite desserts. If the kids are around, though, it's like the movie title *Gone in 60 Seconds!*

SERVES
4

PREP
10 MINS

SAUTE
0 MINS

PRESSURE COOK
0 MINS

RELEASE
N/A

TOTAL COOK TIME
0 MINS

865 CALS

DOM'S MINI BANOFFEE PIES

A cheesecake-style crust, bananas, caramel and plenty of cream - what's not to love? This is the dream recipe for using up that can of condensed milk that you just pressure cooked (see page 212). Dom made these on repeat when working as a hotel chef, but his complaint was the long, long wait for the caramel in the pan of boiling water. It would often take 4 hours! But make caramel in the pressure cooker, and it's done in a fraction of the time.

100g/3½oz digestive biscuits/ graham crackers
28g/1oz/⅛ cup unsalted butter, melted
3 medium bananas
1 x 397g/14oz sweetened condensed milk turned into caramel (see page 212)

FOR DECORATING

240ml/8½fl oz/1 cup double/heavy cream
½ tsp vanilla extract
2 pinches of ground cinnamon
1 tbsp chocolate chips or roughly chopped dark chocolate

01 Tip the biscuits into a bowl, then use the end of a rolling pin to bash them to crumbs. Pour the melted butter into the bowl and mix well until it's all combined.

02 Divide the mixture between 4 ramekins. Press the mixture down with the back of a spoon or a spatula until level. Place the ramekins on a tray in the freezer for 10 minutes to harden up a bit.

03 Peel and slice the bananas, then add to a bowl with the caramel. Stir to coat, then spoon the banana mixture into the ramekins over the biscuit crumb.

04 Pour the cream into a clean bowl and whisk with an electric hand mixer. Add the vanilla and cinnamon, and mix again. Continue until the cream has completely thickened.

05 Add a fluted nozzle to a piping/pastry bag, then add the whipped cream and push it down. Pipe the cream over the banana caramel in the ramekins. Finally, sprinkle the tops with chocolate chips. You can store them in the fridge for later or enjoy now.

SERVES
8

PREP
8 MINS

SAUTE
0 MINS

PRESSURE
COOK
20 MINS

RELEASE
QPR

TOTAL
COOK TIME
20 MINS

729 CALS

KEY LIME PIE

Limes, egg yolks and condensed milk are the base ingredients for a key lime pie. It's like the lazy version of a cheesecake and tastes so good.

255g/9oz any biscuits/cookies (we use ginger biscuits)
75g/2¾oz/⅓ cup unsalted butter, melted
4 large egg yolks
2 × 397g/14oz cans sweetened condensed milk
1 tsp vanilla extract
Zest and juice of 4 limes

FOR DECORATING

240ml/8½fl oz/1 cup double/heavy cream
Zest and juice of 2 limes
1 tbsp vanilla extract
2 tbsp icing/confectioners' sugar

01 Tip the biscuits into a bowl, then use the end of a rolling pin to bash them to crumbs. Pour the melted butter into the bowl and mix well until it's all combined.

02 Tip the mixture into a springform tin/pan (ours is 18cm/7in). Press the mixture down with the back of a spoon or a spatula until level. Place in the freezer to set for 20 minutes whilst you make your filling.

03 Add the egg yolks, condensed milk and vanilla to a mixing bowl. Beat with a wooden spoon until creamy and well mixed. Stir in the lime zest and juice.

04 Pour the mixture over the biscuit base, levelling it with the back of your spoon. Cover the tin with foil.

05 Pour 360ml/12fl oz/1½ cups cold water into the cooking pot and add the trivet/rack.

06 Lower the key lime pie carefully onto the trivet. Secure the pressure cooker lid and set the valve to sealing. Pressure cook for 20 minutes, followed by a quick pressure release.

07 Open the lid, but leave the pie to cool in the pot. Finally, lift it out, remove the foil and leave it to rest in the fridge overnight.

08 To decorate, pour the cream into a mixing bowl and whisk with an electric hand mixer. Add the lime juice, vanilla and icing sugar, and mix again. Continue until the cream has completely thickened.

09 Add a fluted nozzle to a piping/pastry bag, then add the cream and push it down. Pipe the cream around the edges of the pie, then sprinkle with the lime zest to serve.

Squeezing the Limes Sometimes you can get really juicy limes, and the next time you buy them there's none. Aim for 2½ tablespoons lime juice in total. If you don't have much juice, use an extra lime in the recipe.

Spare Egg Whites Use the leftover egg whites to make the egg white bites on page 32.

INDEX

D

E

F

G

LOTS OF THANK YOUS

It takes a team to make a cookbook and we are so appreciative of everyone who has helped us take this book from a vague idea to beautifully photographed recipes, in-depth recipe instructions and a list of recipes that truly help the pressure cooker beginner.

Our community Without you we wouldn't have bought our first Instant Pot pressure cooker all those years ago. It gave us the amazing passion for pressure cooking that we didn't even know we had. You have always let us know what help you needed, and these same questions have shaped the introduction and the recipes themselves. We also appreciate every social media share and every video thumbs up, as it all helps us grow and be seen.

To the members of kitchen gadgets club We love how passionate you are about the pressure cooker and other gadgets, and how you tell us which recipes you'd like to make next. You have helped us grow and change direction in the last year.

Rudi our vision board I have loved every story you have shared about a childhood growing up with pressure cooking – about the pressure cookers you've had, what you loved and how your mum fed a family using the pressure cooker. Thanks for all of the recipes you translated from German to English for me, they have really taught me so much about the history of pressure cooking. I love that you're my vision board and we hope you love how we have turned your stories into a book.

To Mr Baker We miss you. You went to heaven during our first book and here we are having made another three without you by our side. I dedicate the pork chops in this book to you.

To Kyle our eldest boy Our original taste tester, our video editor, our social media designer and our 'we need ingredients from the supermarket fast' assistant. Thank you for all your help again on our fourth book. Although, I think your favourite part was eating all the food! You make us so proud and we love the adult you have become.

To Sofia our girl We love how organised you are. We love how talented you are. You are so helpful and we couldn't have done this book without you. You never complained, not once when we needed help in the kitchen. A true angel. I am so proud of you and can't believe you are now in big school – we started our pressure cooker adventure when you were just a toddler.

To Jorge our youngest boy You may only be ten, but that doesn't stop you getting stuck in – from making the sushi with your sister to telling me my food was the best ever. (Feel free to keep saying that!) You're so smart, so passionate about what you do and make Mummy and Daddy proud every single day.

Sarah our recipe tester Thank you for all your encouragement and giving me positive thoughts when I've had a bad day, and for cleaning a zillion gadgets and never complaining. We will forever remember you and this book for recipe testing our sushi and being so good at it.

Claire my bestie There is not enough space here for me to thank you for everything that you do for us and the amazing support you provide. You're such a kind, wonderful person and thank you for all the emotional support you provide – trying all our recipes, telling us what recipes you love the most, and picking the kids up from school when I'm running behind on a recipe.

To our agent Clare Thank you for all your help – I can't believe we are now at four books. We love how you believed in us and we are proud to call you our agent.

Denise our publisher We finally got a chance to meet, yet here we are creating book four! It has been a pleasure working with you again and introducing you to the wonderful world of pressure cooking. I will forever be grateful and dedicate the bean salad to you. Thank you for taking a chance on us and for letting us share our passion with you for the electric pressure cooker. Your advice and experience have shaped our cookbooks for the better.

Nicky Thank you for all your feedback, coming to the photoshoot, even when you were under the weather, my super-sized recipe print outs and letting us use your expertise to achieve the best photographs.

Jo Wow, how did I get such a lovely editor? I feel honoured to be working with you again on another book. You have taught me so much about editing and made me a better writer in the process. I love your ideas and how you cope so well with last-minute edits and requests to make that important text fit.

Sophie In our last book you were the assistant and now you're our food stylist. We loved working with you on another cookbook. It has been fascinating watching you as our food stylist and the unique style you bring. And you were still smiling, even when we had a last-minute recipe tweak.

Sadie Thank you for being our assistant and letting me see what was missing in teaching beginners about the pressure cooker.

Dan We've had you as part of our team now on three books and one cooking guide – we love your photography and your attention to detail in getting the photo just right.

Georgie Wow, our fourth cookbook together. I don't want anyone but you designing our books. You're so super talented, make sure all the text we want fits, think outside the box and make every design look so original.

Alison When I walked into our business group almost five years ago, I never expected to meet someone as great as you. You're such a talented photographer and I just love the product photos that you've made for us.

Julie Without you there wouldn't have been any cookbooks. You gave me the get up and go and showed me that anything is possible. You were my shoulder to cry on and I am so lucky to call you my friend. I have loved your transformation over the last few years and I am looking forward to watching you as your new business grows.

ABOUT THE AUTHORS

Sam and Dom Milner live in East Yorkshire in the north of England with their three kids, Kyle, Sofia and Jorge. Their home is oven free and surrounded with all their favourite kitchen gadgets. Sam met Dom when he worked as a sous chef more than 25 years ago and they love cooking together with their gadgets.

For more kitchen gadget recipes, handy tips, recipe videos and easy-to-follow tutorials check out:

KITCHENGADGETSCLUB.COM

If you have any pressure cooker recipe questions or just want to say hi then our socials are:

- **thekitchengadgetsclub** (Instagram)
- **kitchengadgetsclub** (TikTok)
- **thekitchengadgetsclub** (Facebook)
- **kitchengadgetsclub** (YouTube)

ALSO FROM SAM & DOM MILNER

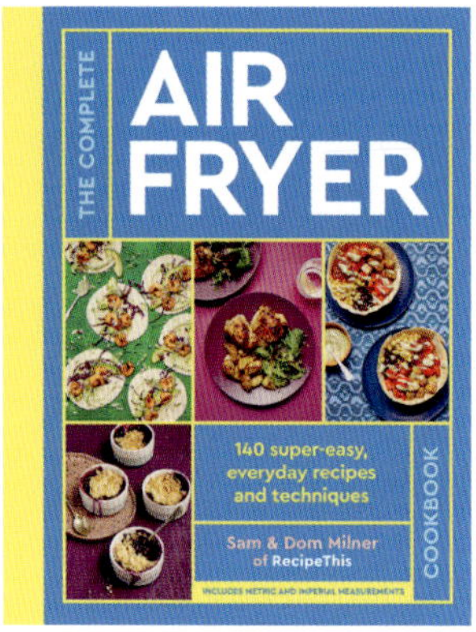

Do you also have an air fryer in your kitchen?
Then check out our beginner-friendly air fryer cookbooks
along with our air fryer time and temperature guide.

Do you have the machine that does it all? Or several gadgets in your kitchen? Then you will love our multicooker book. It's packed to bursting with everyday dishes, together with a recipes-by-function index, with recipes featuring pressure cooking, air frying, steam air frying and our favourite – combining pressure cooking and air frying.

And our *Complete Multicooker Cooking Guide* provides fully tested times and temperatures for every setting.